T0316557

Cambridge Elements

Elements in Global Urban History
edited by
Michael Goebel
Graduate Institute Geneva
Tracy Neumann
Wayne State University
Joseph Ben Prestel
Freie Universität Berlin

REAL ESTATE AND GLOBAL URBAN HISTORY

Alexia Yates
University of Manchester

CAMBRIDGE
UNIVERSITY PRESS

CAMBRIDGE
UNIVERSITY PRESS

University Printing House, Cambridge CB2 8BS, United Kingdom

One Liberty Plaza, 20th Floor, New York, NY 10006, USA

477 Williamstown Road, Port Melbourne, VIC 3207, Australia

314–321, 3rd Floor, Plot 3, Splendor Forum, Jasola District Centre,
New Delhi – 110025, India

103 Penang Road, #05–06/07, Visioncrest Commercial, Singapore 238467

Cambridge University Press is part of the University of Cambridge.

It furthers the University's mission by disseminating knowledge in the pursuit of
education, learning, and research at the highest international levels of excellence.

www.cambridge.org
Information on this title: www.cambridge.org/9781108797115
DOI: 10.1017/9781108850551

First published 2021

A catalogue record for this publication is available from the British Library.

ISBN 978-1-108-79711-5 PAPERBACK
ISSN 2632-3206 (online)
ISSN 2632-3192 (print)

Real Estate and Global Urban History

Elements in Global Urban History

DOI: 10.1017/9781108850551
First published online: June 2021

Alexia Yates

Author for correspondence: Alexia Yates, alexia.yates@manchester.ac.uk

Abstract: Real estate – capitalist private property in land and buildings – is the ground of modern cities, materially, politically, and economically. It is foundational to their development and core to much theoretical work on the urban environment. It is also a central, pressing matter of political contestation in contemporary cities. Yet it remains largely without a history. This Element examines the modern city as a propertied space, defining real estate as a technology of (dis) possession and using this definition to move across scales of analysis, from the local spatiality of particular built spaces to the networks of legal, political, and economic imperatives that constitute property and operate at national and international levels. This combination of territorial embeddedness with more wide-ranging institutional relationships charts a route to an urban history that allows the city to speak as a global agent and artefact without dispensing with the role of states and local circumstance.

Keywords: real estate, cities, political economy, urban theory, global history

ISBNs: 9781108797115 (PB), 9781108850551 (OC)
ISSNs: 2632-3206 (online), 2632-3192 (print)

Contents

1 Introduction: The Case for Real Estate

In the leadup to a global financial crisis and economic depression, Montréal was among the first places where a real estate boom became a bubble. Within a few years, Rome followed; credit from northern Italian banks (backed by French finance) flooded into the capital, driving up land prices before contracting and leaving in its wake partially finished buildings and bankrupt owners. Simultaneously, Paris, Lyon, and Nice, linked by the same financial flows, saw frenetic speculative construction and collapses in building prices in the span of only a few years. Police observers in Paris strove vainly to comprehend how rents went up even as building was incessant – a phenomenon 'in strict contradiction with the laws of supply and demand' – while the municipal council concluded that 'in no other period has the dynamic of construction and demolition enacted such significant changes in the condition of land in such a short span of time'.[1] In Stockholm, more dwellings were constructed in eight or nine years than had been produced in the previous seventy-five. Real estate in Winnipeg and Los Angeles, booster cities of the North American West, boomed and busted at the same time. In Shanghai and Hong Kong, real estate was one of many speculative assets that tumbled as foreign credit tightened. It took some time for price declines and foreclosures to play out, but by the time this round of real estate booms had subsided in 1889, many of the world's advanced capitalist economies were well settled into the 'long depression' of the late nineteenth century. Surveying the unprecedented unemployment and decline in wages and prices of this depression – and coming in for their share of the blame – real estate brokers and developers in cities around the world came to a new awareness of the national and global factors shaping their field of operations (Burley, 1988; Chuan, 1979; Di Martino, 2012; Forsell, 2006; Glaeser, 2013; Kang, 1993).

This account likely conjures images of the real estate bubble and financial crisis that led to the Great Recession of the early twenty-first century (Shiller, 2005). That crisis sprang from years of easy credit to homebuyers facilitated by thick networks of securitization, by which individual mortgages were packaged into asset-backed securities whose risks and income streams were circulated and re-assembled between a range of global investors (Fligstein and Goldstein, 2010). Mortgages, in the words of political scientist Kathe Newman (2009), had become the widgets of the post-industrial United States: mass-produced building blocks that form the basic material of the

---

[1] Archives de la Préfecture de Police de Paris, BA 486: Rapport, Commissariat de Police des Quartiers de la Santé et du Petit-Montrouge, 19 juin 1882; Conseil Municipal de Paris, Rapport, présenté par M. Alfred Lamouroux, au nom de la 1re Commission, sur la valeur locative actuelle des propriétés bâties de la ville de Paris, en exécution de la loi du 8 août 1885 (Paris: 1888), 25.

financialized economy. By the early 2000s, the demand for these securities was such that increasing numbers of mortgages were offered to candidates who would not typically gain access to such credit – so-called sub-prime clients – further fuelling what had already been decades of housing price increases. When these new mortgages began resulting in higher than predicted levels of default, the by-now massive and global industry of mortgage-backed securities was severely destabilized. Banks and other investor funds found themselves over leveraged, while individual homeowners began losing homes, housing value, and economic security. This was a crisis within and across scales: of individual households, of national banks and government bodies, of international investment circuits. While accounts of the crisis often privilege the national or international scale in their focus on government regulation and global pools of money, cities and their political economy were central to the unfolding of the mortgage boom and bust (Marcinkoski, 2015; Aalbers, 2012).

This juxtaposition of a late nineteenth-century and early twenty-first-century contagion of real estate bubbles is more than a feint to suggest the relevance of real estate and its history for contemporary urban dynamics. It does demonstrate that real estate, as a physical entity, a field of interests, and a mode of capital accumulation, has been a central force in cities throughout the modern era (a period identified here with the long-nineteenth, twentieth, and twenty-first centuries). It demonstrates, too, that assets that are extremely local and place bound – like housing and neighbourhood land, drenched in the use value of individual owners and residents – have long been shaped by national and international movements of capital. In other words, that there is a deeper history to footloose capital's urban predation and production than that typically identified with contemporary globalization and neoliberalism. But the juxtaposition is also intended to highlight the necessity of granting real estate a historicity in our accounts of the urban. Reckoning with what are, as presented, two similar international crises separated by more than a century opens challenging and fruitful terrain for historians of cities who seek to move their analyses across broader scales of time and space. What might such repetition tell us about the nature of urban development, and the types of historical inquiry required to make sense of it? But the distinctions between these moments, which would be revealed by deeper study, are also vital. The real estate crises of the 1880s were not identical to the mortgage-fuelled calamities of the 2000s: the former did not enjoy the unity provided by contemporary marketization; individual homeownership played practically no role (though it was more influential in the North American cases); in most instances, urban bubbles coincided rather than shared common origins.

These differences in the treatment and function of real estate in the modern city – the sharp divergences that underlie shared language of 'building fevers' and 'speculative booms' – demand the critical attention of historians. Capitalist private property in land and buildings – real estate – is the ground of modern cities, materially, politically, and economically. It is foundational to their development and core to much theoretical work on the urban environment. It is also a central, pressing matter of political contestation in contemporary cities. Yet it remains largely without a history. As historian LeeAnn Lands writes in her study of real estate and working class housing in turn-of-the-century Atlanta, 'historians and other scholars often referred to neighborhoods and housing as having "formed" around rail junctions, factory locations, and the like, as if they were a natural outgrowth of a nearby transportation nexus or workplace, or as if workers themselves merely called on squatters' rights and settled in the most convenient location' (Lands, 2002, p.547). The actions of developers, of owners who make up urban 'growth machines', of ordinary people as they navigate property markets and their changing regimes of commoditization – all these too often exist in a curious black box, from which unchanging categories such as 'speculators', 'developers', 'landlords', and 'renters' issue without significant historical assessment. Yet in fact, these groups shift, align, and act in historically specific ways, even if their evolution under modern capitalism enjoys an overall coherence.

If urban history has frequently neglected to critically engage with real estate, the same can be said of new histories of capitalism. These histories tend to privilege studies of finance, insurance, and money – the world of risk, probability, speculation, and capital flows – over the purportedly more fixed terrain of land, patrimony, and real property (Yates, 2019b). This is partially explained by present-day economic concerns, and informed by a fascination for the technological and mathematical mechanics of modern capitalist practice. In contrast to the dynamic, globe-spanning transactions of modern finance, the long-term stability of real estate, its material durability and its fixity in space, seem to embody a 'traditional' world destined for eclipse. Historical studies of the globalizing modern economy are similarly little preoccupied with unmovable territory left in the wake of flows of commodities, capital, and labour, while cultural and social histories of the global bourgeoisie – a class for which property arguably constituted a defining asset, aspiration, and ideology – also bypass the subject (Abbenhuis and Morrell, 2020; Dejung, et al., 2019; Topik and Wells, 2012).[2] To be sure, longer term studies of the evolution of wealth

---

[2] It should be noted, however, that some important recent research on globalization engages with the ways that states and empires 'territorialize' their economic and governmental regimes (Ballantyne and Burton, 2012). In a summary contribution to a new volume on the history of

have established the declining significance of real property as a component of national income throughout the eighteenth and nineteenth centuries – however, the global rise of individual home ownership following the Second World War reverses that trend, and also initiates the first period of sustained increases in property prices for several centuries (Eichholtz, 1997; Piketty, 2014).

Happily, other disciplines have proven more ready to tackle real estate as a historically-specific element of modern cities and economies. In urban studies, critical geography, and economic sociology, the gyrations of real estate and financial markets in the early twenty-first century have generated considerable research into the role of real estate capital in the financialization of the global economy, as well as into the way its fallout has changed the global urban landscape (Aalbers, 2008; Fields, 2017; Gotham, 2006; Kaika and Ruggiero, 2013; Sassen, 2008). This literature has drawn on the insights of Marxist geographers Henri Lefebvre (2003) and David Harvey (discussed in more detail below) in order to focus attention on the role of real estate as a circuit for capital accumulation. Informed by such research, as well as by a diverse assemblage of historical studies, this volume argues that real estate enjoys a particular ability to both affect and illuminate fundamental processes of urbanization.

Understanding urban real estate as an object of historical inquiry requires reflection on the meaning and analytic work performed by the term. In his study of race and real estate in south Florida, historian Nathan D. B. Connolly defines real estate succinctly as 'land turned into property for the sake of further capital investment' (Connolly, 2014, p.6). This definition serves the purposes of a modern historian reasonably well. It aligns key elements of the real estate package – land as a non-human-made precondition, property as a legal institution, and capital as the means and end of real estate's existence – but avoids collapsing them. It captures real estate's invented and transformative capacity ('land *turned into*') and incorporates recognition of its future orientation ('*further* capital investment'). Nevertheless, some refinement can improve the utility of the term for the urban historian and further emphasize its historical specificity.

Real estate is at once an old concept and a decidedly modern referent. A common-law term dating from at least the seventeenth century (though the notion of 'real property' is still older), it designates a category of property separate from chattel or other personal estate, such as money, merchandise, or other goods. It takes its meaning – in legal, but also cultural and political terms – from the tangible and immovable nature of land and buildings. Such property is

---

capitalism, Sven Beckert acknowledges the need for the field to deal more forthrightly with the history of the countryside, and includes land as a key resource whose commoditization demands more attention (Beckert, 2016).

'real' and protected in a way that movable, personal property is not. This holds true in both the common law and civil code systems. The French term for real estate, *immobilier*, captures the division in the Napoleonic Code between the civil realm – into which immovable, real property falls – and the commercial – the realm of movable goods and personalty. In contrast to the venerable standing of the concept in the major legal systems which came to cover much of the globe, in common parlance 'real estate' as we deploy it today was not much used before the mid-nineteenth century. Legal discourse, political debate, economic disquisition, and those who worked in the management and traffic of 'real estate' referred to property, estates, buildings, and land, rather than the more general category (Fitz-Gibbon, 2018; Yates, 2015).

The shift to a more generalized usage of real estate in today's commercialized sense is a multi-causal process, with important national variation, but which owes much to modern imperialism. Colonial frontiers and imperial cities were spaces in which property, from the perspective of colonizing authorities, was born as real estate (Bhandar, 2018) (Figure 1). This was a material boon for the colonizers, who sought to accumulate capital through dispossession of existing owners, occupants, and users of land. It was also a discursive move that allowed a sort of hierarchy between *real* 'real property' that existed in the metropole and the inferior 'real estate', shorn of political and cultural privileges, of the colonized territory. Indeed, real estate in colonized territories was a lever that helped construct a hierarchy of personal estates – such as the differentiated legal regimes for Muslim subjects in French Algeria – conducive to imperial governance (Surkis, 2019).

Making property in the empire was frequently about making what we might call commodity real property: property that could easily circulate, as liquid as other forms of capital. In colonial North America, for instance, as legal historian Claire Priest shows, the English parliament's Debt Recovery Act of 1732 transformed the character of real property in its North American possessions, rendering it much closer to chattel than its metropolitan equivalent by degrading real property's privileges and protections vis-à-vis creditors (Priest, 2006). In the nineteenth century, systems such as the Torrens system of land registration, which combined new techniques of surveying and registration to mobilize land and maximize its (financial) productivity, were developed and deployed across imperial territories, first in British colonies and then throughout the French empire and into diverse parts of North America and East Asia. Other empires studied and emulated European measures. The Ottoman Empire's Land Law of 1858 provides a well-known example of imperial reaction, as European models of individual ownership were adopted as a method of stimulating economic growth and centralizing governance (Islamoglu, 2004; Mundy, 2004). Japan

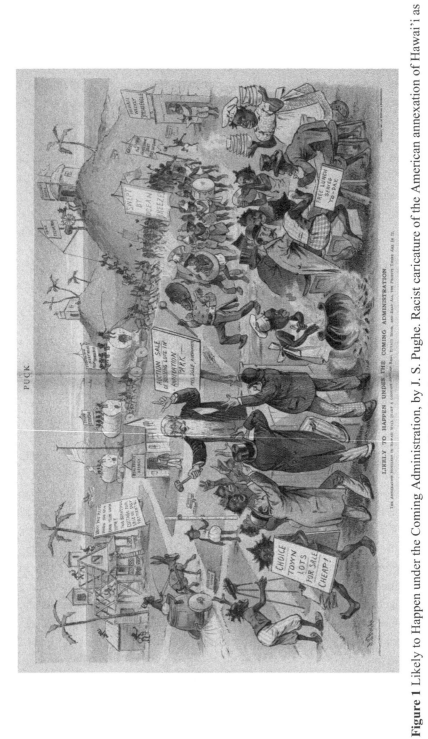

Figure 1 Likely to Happen under the Coming Administration, by J. S. Pughe. Racist caricature of the American annexation of Hawai'i as a (fraudulent) real estate boom.

Puck vol. 40, no. 1038 (27 January 1897). Library of Congress.

acted similarly in Korea at the turn of the twentieth century, setting about renovating the land registration system on the European imperial model in order to open up Korean land to foreign investment (Lee, 2014). (In other instances, such as land reforms in Qing China, similar methods were pursued without the spur of European models (Macauley, 2001).) While enthusiasts of these rationalizing and maximizing methods hoped such techniques could migrate back to the European core, with the exception of English governance in Ireland such experiments were delayed for decades. Real estate, as it was born in this global context, was a mode and rationale of extraction and dispossession, crucially distinct from the political virtues of stewardship and autonomy represented by real property in the metropole (Grossi, 1981; Hoppit, 2011).

Our use of the term real estate, then, has this modern history embedded within it. Centring this history is of prime importance for the study of the contemporary city, which is perpetually shaped by dynamics of possession (for the wealthy, for settlers, for gentrifiers . . .) and dispossession (for the poor, for indigenous, for the displaced . . .), and is one of the reasons why real estate is a central concept and entity for any global urban history (Blatman-Thomas and Porter, 2019; Everett, 2019; Maggor, 2017). In contrast to the more general language often used by urban historians to refer to land and buildings in the urban setting – terms like 'landscape', 'urban fabric', or 'built environment' – real estate presents a specific set of relationships for historical inquiry. As a term with a deep legal history, it draws attention to the bundles of rights that constitute ownership, to the fact that property is a set of relationships (more than only a 'thing' possessed), among which the most important are the relationships of definition and enforcement instituted by the state (Banner, 2011). These relations constitute real estate as a social fact, elevating it from the lot for sale or apartment for rent and revealing its status as a terrain of social production and contestation. When understood this way, a focus on real estate does not risk reducing the study of the city to a study of urban economics, nor does it risk neglecting people in favour of property.

At the same time as real estate brings a much broader web of relations into focus, both its history and everyday usage retains an emphasis on the 'real', which also does important work for urban history. In particular, the material and tangible aspects of real estate, which necessarily exist in a particular place, invite close analyses of local spatiality, of specific structures and the lived experiences they shape. This is the terrain of the everyday, of the scale of interaction at which global processes make themselves felt, are negotiated, sometimes transformed (Sandoval-Strausz and Kwak, 2017). It offers scope for actor-centred stories that extend beyond (while not excluding) influential policymakers, legislators, or planners. The territorial embeddedness of real estate – which is also a temporal embeddedness, as land and buildings can outlast owners and users – combines with more wide-ranging institutional relationships to chart a route to an urban history that allows the city to speak as a global agent and artefact without dispensing with the role of states and local circumstance.

None of this is to say that other geographical or architectural types, or the potent analytic categories of space and place, lack value or will not feature in the account that follows. Neighbourhood, apartment building, home, zone, suburb, gated community, ghetto – these are themselves social facts with critical impact in cities as well as proven analytic capacity (Topalov et al., 2010; Harris and Vorms, 2017). It is simply to point out that there are some advantages for our urban histories from thinking of real estate in the way just outlined – as an enhancement and historicization of our thinking on the propertied city – and engaging with it as a particular mode of organizing and analysing the urban (Blomley, 2014). And of course, urban historians have long done so, even if not as part of a self-defined research agenda. Part of the goal of what follows is to synthesize this literature, reviewing the place of real estate in urban history and theory.

Sketched in these terms, some concluding observations are in order on real estate's capacity to travel, as an object of analysis, in time and space. Does its constitution through a modern history of value production and extraction limit its application to the recent past, or to the geographic and economic terrain of contemporary capitalism? A rich historiography concerning the economics of urban property relations in medieval and early modern cities suggests scope for real estate's analytic relevance across time periods (Łozowksi, 2018; Raff, 2013; Yates, 2013). Yet this application, most pronounced in economic history, involves a certain historical flattening, and little beyond real estate's prices generally attracts attention. Real estate is the product of a modern discourse, a way of building, appreciating, and experiencing the city in a distinct historical moment. While elements of its contemporary formulation appear and are operative in a range of historical contexts, its current articulation – and the salience of that articulation – must be tested for applicability in earlier moments rather than assumed.

Similar care is required of pursuing real estate beyond the capitalist city. What, for example, of the dynamics of cities and urbanism under the socialist regimes of the twentieth century? How far does it make sense to speak of real estate in 1970s Beijing, 1960s Bucharest, or 1930s Moscow, all contexts in which the role of market forces in the production of urban space is subject to clear limits and interventions? The extent to which state socialism produced sufficiently distinct and coherent urban settings to grant analytic traction to the notion of a 'socialist city' continues to be debated (French and Hamilton, 1979; Hirt, 2013; Zarecor, 2018).[3] Certainly, there were political and spatial attributes of the very real revolutionary projects for socialist urban modernity that suggest 'real estate' requires substantial qualification in these settings. In the Soviet Union, urban land and buildings were municipalized (in separate decrees) starting as early as December 1917, halting private transactions in real estate and centralizing processes of management and distribution (O'Donnell, 2014). The establishment of the Eastern Bloc post-1945 was accompanied by similar measures, though great variety persisted between the form and extent of nationalization in cities across the region (Chelcea, 2012; Serban, 2019; Zarecor, 2011). Examples (again, with significant differences) can be extended to include cities in Maoist China or Havana after 1959 (Rutheiser, 2003; Yeh and Wu, 1996).

In these contexts, the role of real estate as a mode of capital accumulation and of private property as a privileged platform of urban politics – both markers of the 'capitalist city' – were significantly reduced. Yet they were never fully eliminated. Socialist regimes shared and even amplified the impulse evident in post-war Western European cities to deploy the production and distribution of urban space to construct new citizens and new state-society relations (Föllmer and Smith, 2015). For the USSR, research by historian Mark Smith (2010) has revealed that private ownership of real property persisted, maintaining a significant place in the planning and practice of socialist cities, even if its relationship to the broader economy's regimes of production was altered as its role in the reproduction of labour was reinforced (Harris, 2013). More broadly, 'socialist cities' offer vital empirical cases of the making and unmaking of markets and of the multiple forms of the politics of dispossession embedded in real estate as an object of analysis. And recent research in these contexts exemplifies how an attention to real estate can destabilize and transform conventional chronologies – for example, by revealing the longer history of contests over the public nature of municipal land before the imposition of Soviet measures in Warsaw, or by tracing the elements of socialist urban planning that endure and support contemporary neoliberal development regimes (Kusiak, 2019; Zarecor, 2018).

Having worked in this section to make the case for real estate's potential as an entry point to a historically rich assemblage of places, things, and relationships in the modern city, the following discussion surveys existing historiography on real estate and the city, before offering a re-reading of urban theory through

---

[3] A forthcoming Element in Global Urban History by Katherine Zubovich addresses the socialist city.

a real estate lens. The final section offers case histories that speak to two of real estate's defining attributes: first, to its role as an engine of capital accumulation, through a brief history of the emergence of the idea and institutions of real estate markets; second, to its role as a legal technology of fixity and embeddedness, and its implications for the study of urban cultures and politics. Without claiming that real estate does not come with its own occlusions, the Element argues that its particular capacity to forge communication between scales of analysis and across realms of social life make it an invaluable tool – and terrain – of inquiry for both the urban and global historian.

2 Real Estate and the Historiography of the City

Real estate, in a basic sense, is everywhere in the history of the city. It is the land and cement dwellings that comprise the *favela*, the filled terrain that extends Bombay's territory, the reclaimed cemeteries that provide foundations for Singapore's high-rises, the self-built homes of Toronto's suburban peripheries. In urban historiography, however, real estate as mode of accumulation is unevenly addressed, with the consequence that it frequently drops from view; it becomes a simple material backdrop – a house, a street, a suburb – to the social, political, and cultural dramas of urbanization. Certainly, a vein of now classic research in urban history provides thoroughgoing accounts of urban development organized around the politics and economics of real estate. This research focused chiefly on cities of England and the United States and was driven by an interest in the material process and shape of urbanization. It combined local studies – such as Sam Bass Warner, Jr.'s (1978, 1968) on the privatized growth of Boston and Philadelphia – with national examinations – such as Kenneth Jackson's (1985) research on suburbanization – along with research on private development itself (Daunton, 1983; Doucet and Weaver, 1991; Dyos, 1982; Rodger, 2002; Weiss, 1987). Yet the advocacy of important researchers like Warner, who enjoined urban historians in the 1970s to train their focus on speculation and ownership – 'the Registry of Deeds rather than the Building Department' – went largely unheeded (Warner, 1978, p.vii). Particular fields, like the history of housing and the history of suburban development, treat buildings and development as a core subject matter, while not consistently addressing these as real estate as such (Fourcaut, 2000; Harris, 1996; Hayden, 1981; Jacobs, 2015; Lewinnek, 2014; Wright, 1983). Architectural history is also an important source of research on the professional development of builders and real estate developers, with recent scholarship increasingly centring these actors in the production of 'entrepreneurial vernaculars' that populate contemporary cityscapes (Stevens, 2016; Loeb, 2001). This historiography (in English) is richest with regard to the Anglo-American context, but important new research projects on the global dimensions of suburbanization have expanded the field of inquiry considerably (Harris and Lehrer, 2018; Phelps, 2017).

Real estate remains notably absent elsewhere, in areas where it may otherwise appear crucially important, such as the history of planning and urban design. As economist Helen Monchow observed in 1928 in one of the earliest works in land economics, 'From the standpoint of controlling development the pattern of our modern cities is determined largely by the activities of two groups, the realtors and the city planners' (Monchow, 1928, p.3). In subsequent historiography, real estate functions as the unexamined 'other' against which planners, the professional managers of space and spatial practice, are aligned; it is the untamed, illegible, and backward mode of city-making with which progressive histories can dispense. (Never mind that the real estate market is among the most powerful, novel forces for giving discipline and order, particularly along racial and class lines, to the modern city, and so in many respects the antithesis of chaotic and antiquated.) A recent essay on real estate development in the *Oxford Handbook of Urban Planning* cites urban studies scholar Anne Haila (1998), observing that 'real estate has not gained popularity as a topic in urban studies. The topic has been left to real estate economists who are mostly interested in developing models as guides for diversification of real estate portfolios' (Gharney, 2012). In fact, early icons of urban planning, such as Ebenezer Howard or Tony Garnier, gave deep consideration to issues such as the municipalization of land and to forms like land trusts that would remove land from the speculative development churn, though practical interventions with such mechanisms were limited and their concerns in this area have been little studied (Hertweck, 2020). Recent contributions to global and transnational approaches to urban planning accentuate this absence, as narratives of intellectual exchange and circulation leave divergent (national) political economies of real estate unexplored (Klemek, 2011; Wakeman, 2016); case study approaches are, however, beginning to reinsert private enterprise as a key accomplice of post-war urban redevelopment (Verlaan, 2019, 2020; Kefford, 2020). Real estate's submersion in the private realm also contributes to its elision in urban history, which is overwhelmingly focused on public space and public governance. Real estate, in contrast, can be construed as doubly private: in addition to being situated analytically in the arena of business, commerce, and private interest, it is closely connected to the residential, privatized spaces of the city. These spaces are frequently feminized, and occupy an ambiguous location in urban history (Marcus, 1999; Yates, 2019a).

Yet real estate's operations and functions are not purely an affair of the private realm. Rather, real estate occupies a central role in urban history as a technology of governance. Real estate has been the means and end of the city, in evolving ways, since the early modern period. As historian Hendrik Hartog shows in his study of the corporation of the city of New York in the eighteenth and nineteenth centuries, municipalities in the British Atlantic were born as property managers. Royal charters granted property for the purposes of government, and it was through the administration of the private property of the chartered corporation that city governments managed urban development. As Hartog writes, 'The proper business of the corporation was the management, care, and disposal of the real estate it owned' (Hartog, 1983, p.40). As cities developed into the nineteenth century, the *raison d'être* of the municipality continued to be property management, with the difference that by the 1820s and 1830s priority was given to the private property of urban residents. As Elizabeth Blackmar explains in her social history of real property relations in New York City, by this period the city came to be understood as an engine to improve real property's exchange values, and city officials 'rhetorically constructed an entrepreneurial public that identified its collective interest as aggregate economic growth and placed the real estate market at the centre of local economic expansion' (Blackmar, 1985, p.161). From New York and Paris to Stockholm and Berlin, the privatized city was a city organized by and for private property (Everett, 2019; Forsell, 2006; Roncayolo, 2002). Public improvements were geared to the enhancement of real estate's exchange value, and most of the betterment values that followed from public expenditures accrued to private property owners.

Cities in varied legal and geographic contexts demonstrated similar tendencies. In Paris in the late-nineteenth century, the municipal government – elected for the first time from 1871 – enjoyed its widest scope for action in the management of city property, which became a training ground for the craft of municipal governance. Yet at the same time, liberal economists cautioned city officials against acting like the private corporations who were increasingly prominent in real estate investment and speculation. Managing public property and supporting development in the interests of private proprietorship was appropriate; transforming the municipality into a landlord who would compete with those interests was not. In imperial cities, where one might expect property markets to occupy only marginal roles in the face of authoritarian urban governance, recent research has shown that commoditized real property could serve and direct colonial ambitions. In Delhi following the 1857 rebellion, for example, the British managed the demolition and reconstruction of the city through a state-sponsored speculative real estate bubble, described by Anish

Vanaik as 'a demonstration of colonial statecraft' in which the government articulated its prioritization of the circulation of urban property (Vanaik, 2019, p.26). Land prices and the hazards of speculation also motivated the municipality – governed by imperial administrators and local elites – when it came to designing and initiating development as the city expanded beyond its walls. Faced with seemingly ungoverned land use on the city's periphery, imperial officials developed an urban policy from the early twentieth century that, as Jyoti Hosagrahar (2005) argues, for the first time privileged maximum returns from state-owned land over other urban priorities. For different reasons springing from its status as a colonial free port, the city government of Hong Kong pursued a 'high land price policy', driving speculative development as a compensation for otherwise constrained municipal finances. When combined with the British government's support for Chinese property ownership in the city – a strategy intended to cement the stability of the imperial regime – late nineteenth-century Hong Kong developed through what historian and architecture scholar Cecilia Chu describes as an official 'speculative urbanism', with urban real estate serving as the city's political and economic infrastructure (Chu, 2013). As a tool of imperial governance, real estate served to embed (elite) colonial subjects in the imperial order through webs of legal obligation and self-interest, while at the same time its material organization of the urban milieu could structure and enforce the discriminatory and segregationist requirements of empire.[4]

The history of race and spatial segregation in the urban setting is one area of study in which real estate has been distinctly prioritized and problematized. Real estate's role in racialized uneven development is a phenomenon that has marked cities around the world; in his account of the global history of urban segregation, historian Carl Nightingale suggests that capitalist land markets have become 'the single most important segregationist force in cities today' (Nightingale, 2012, p.7). Scholarship on this subject has for some time been most developed for cities of the United States. The country's distinct racial and urban history, combined with the privatized and entrepreneurial nature of real estate development described above, help explain the strength of this vein of research. (Studies on urban racial segregation in the European context not only contend with different patterns of exclusion, but deal chiefly

---

[4] These studies represent departures from traditional histories of colonial cities, which tend to be studies of official practices of urban development and governance with little place for non-state actors or focus on the economy of property relations (Abu-Lughod, 1980; Çelik, 1997; King, 1976). David Prochaska's (2004) study of Bône (now Annaba) in French Algeria dedicates some attention to the role of land grabbers and speculators, while William Bissell's (2011) study of planning in Zanzibar City takes the messiness, unevenness, and 'chaos' of colonial planning in action as its primary focus.

with the state as producer of social housing.[5]) Important books by Kevin Fox Gotham (2002), LeeAnn Lands (2009), Beryl Satter (2009), David Freund (2007), Nathan D. B. Connolly (2014), and most recently, Keeanga-Yamahtta Taylor (2019), have used the cases of Kansas City, Atlanta, Chicago, Detroit, Miami, and New York to demonstrate how United States housing policy became leashed to the corporate interests of real estate capitalists, for whom discrimination constituted profitable enterprise from the early twentieth century. These works demonstrate that far from being neglected or overlooked, Black working-class communities were central to the practices and profits of the modern real estate industry, at local and national scales. As Satter writes, 'The reason for the decline of so many black urban neighborhoods into slums was not the absence of resources but rather the *riches* that could be drawn from the seemingly poor vein of aged and decrepit housing and hard-pressed but hardworking and ambitious African Americans' (Satter, 2009, p.6). Taylor describes this lucrative, unequal incorporation of Black Americans into systems of housing finance as 'predatory inclusion' (Taylor, 2019, p.5).

This scholarship has changed our understanding of the dynamics of people and property in the modern American metropolis, pivoting attention away from a single-minded focus on suburbanization toward an image of housing production and population churn that incorporates hitherto underappreciated transformations in urban cores and which speaks to the experiences of racially and economically marginalized groups. In the process, it has done much to denaturalize real estate, to move it from a simple artefact of scarce land and market forces to present it instead as a terrain of contestation, a tool, a strategy of construction and reproduction of (unequal) power relations.

Pulling the focus out from the United States and adopting a comparative perspective, similarities in how real estate interests have capitalized on racialized uneven development in cities around the globe become clear. The fortunes formed through housing Black and Latinx families in the urban cores of the twentieth-century US find commonalities with those based on the working-class households that populate the informal settlements of Brazil

---

[5] To illuminate this distinction, perhaps the most well-known scholar of French structures of urban marginality, Loïc Wacquant, does not engage with the role of capitalist housing and development interests in his comparative analysis of advanced marginality in the US 'ghetto' and the French *banlieue*, and the sophisticated unpacking of the French house market as a social structure of the economy by his teacher and collaborator, Pierre Bourdieu, has proven the least impactful of that scholar's influential work (Wacquant, 2008; Bourdieu, 2005). In contrast, Kenny Cupers (2014) offers an exemplary study of French urban planning and marginality that includes significant consideration of real estate development interests.

and India – though certainly, differences in actors, politics, and spatial patterns remain. From Chicago to Mumbai to Rio, such communities may be *marginalized* but are not in fact *marginal* to the social and economic life of the cities in which they are located (Perlman, 1976). Taking seriously the constitutive capacity of real estate to enact *differential dispossession* – or, put differently, its capacity to simultaneously ensure possession and stability (for some people, at some times) by virtue of facilitating dispossession (of other people, at other times) – helps these transnational trends come into view and provides a framework for analysing their processes and politics.

Influenced in part by studies of colonialism and imperial cities, a more globalized approach to real estate's constitution and its contribution to racially differentiated development is beginning to make progress. Nightingale, for instance, provides a genealogy of modern urban real estate markets that locates their origin in imperial ideas of racial distinction and the practical demands of imperial financial interests for moving money between propertied investments in cities of the British empire at the turn of the nineteenth century. Further 'perfections' in the segregationist capacities of urban real estate occurred in the later nineteenth century, when the practice of restrictive covenants travelled between countries as a condition of globalizing real estate investment (Glotzer, 2020). In the years following the Second World War, real estate's most ordinary form, housing, became a pillar of social citizenship in diverse regimes around the world. This intersection of real estate and social rights heightened the often racialized tensions of the 'housing question.' (Argersinger, 2010; Murphy, 2015; Murphy and Hourani, 2013; Nasiali, 2016; Pinto, 2009). Indeed, the housing question itself has escaped the confines of the nation-state. Nancy Kwak (2015) has shown, for instance, how United States policymakers pushed a homeownership agenda globally after the Second World War, promoting the programme as support for democracy and capitalism through their own aid programs and a range of international economic bodies. The globalization of real estate investment has grown apace with the financialization of the economy, and has been shaped in the process by this international political agenda of private ownership as development strategy. The stakes of ownership, possession, enclosure, and occupation in the urban context – the politics of presence and the right to the city – have been raised as a consequence (Desmond, 2016; Rolnik, 2013; Sassen, 2014).

As this summary of the place of real estate in urban historiography indicates, an appreciation of real estate as a technology of governance, mode of accumulation, and terrain of contestation has taken over from an approach that leashed real estate more closely to studies of urban growth. Studies that incorporate real estate as a sector or industry in urban development supply important correctives and reformulations of our understanding of who makes the modern city. Alongside planners or the state, the uncoordinated work of private actors, from builders and property owners to architects, lawyers, and insurance companies, as well as urban residents themselves, who shape the material and economic form of the city as they negotiate its buildings and markets, helps to create new narratives of urban development (Buzzelli and Harris, 2006). But still more instructive are histories that engage with real estate as a social relation and tool of governance and economic production. This approach has been strongly influenced by methods and models of the social sciences, particularly sociology and geography, to which we now turn.

3 Urban Theory, Through the Real Estate Lens

3.1 Real Estate and Theories of Urban Pasts

Real estate and the social science of the city were born together (Hall, 2014; Lees, 1985; Tonkiss, 2005). Starting from the nineteenth century, real estate has provided one of the most influential modes of 'seeing' a city, of divining its evolution and theorizing its organization. To administrators who ordered cadastral surveys to render the income and tax liability of urban property visible to the state, or to late nineteenth-century insurance companies who mapped the risk associated with fire (and later, housing finance), real estate has provided the basis for influential renderings of urban space (Figure 2). These renderings increased in significance as the map shifted in the nineteenth century from a representational artefact to a tool for understanding and manipulating key facets of urban life (Gaudin, 1985; Picon, 2003). The growth in municipal statistics and increasingly sophisticated methods of visual presentation of data toward the end of the century – a golden age of statistical graphics – resulted in impactful volumes like the annual compilations of the municipal statistical service of Paris (established in 1881), which vividly rendered property values, land sales, and construction alongside other quantifiable urban phenomena like transportation volume and mortality (Friendly, 2008).

Private actors, like real estate agents and developers, were important contributors to this growing world of paper representations of urban change.[6] Their maps, schematics of lots for sale, diagrams of building and apartment layouts – all collated in new gazettes and other publications that attested to the construction of local real estate 'markets' – became some of the

---

[6] In characteristic fashion, a recent special section on paper and municipal governance in the *Journal of Urban History* makes no mention of the work of non-state actors. See Lee and Weiss, 2020.

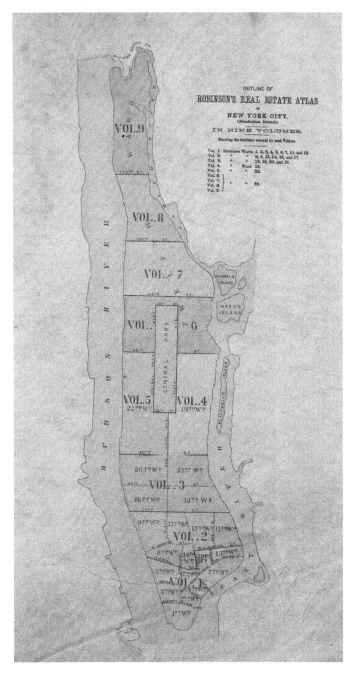

Figure 2 The city rendered as real estate: Outline of Robinson's Real Estate Atlas of New York City (Manhattan Island), 1889.

Lionel Pincus and Princess Firyal Map Division, The New York Public Library Digital Collections. Accessed 7 February 2021. https://digitalcollections.nypl.org/items/a1ec3dd4-57b3-e18d-e040-e00a18064727

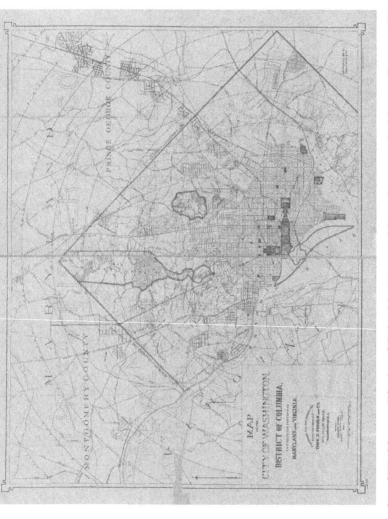

Figure 3 Map of the city of Washington, District of Columbia, 'Prepared for and presented with compliments of Thos. J. Fisher and Co., real estate brokers', 1891.

most familiar representations of cities in circulation (Figures 3 and 4). In Chicago, as historian Elaine Lewinnek (2010) shows, urban boosters published maps that localized areas of current real estate development while at the same time establishing projections of development to come, illustrating the growth of the city as a series of future suburbanizations emanating from the urban core. Their representations helped summon the terrain they imagined into being, building and shaping the development dynamism that would make (some) visions reality. Their city was a real estate phenomenon, motored by private development and individual ownership.

This vernacular urban science produced important sources and approaches for early sociologists and what would soon become known as land economics (Abbott, 1981; Weiss, 2000). The ring models of urban property values discerned and declaimed by realtors in the early-twentieth century were translated, through urban plans and textbooks, into the zonal theory of concentric circles that characterized the Chicago School of sociology's model of urban growth. As Lewinnek argues regarding Ernest Burgess, a leading member of Chicago's 'ecological' school, 'Burgess adapted a half-century of realtors' maps and codified them in a model of abstraction and urban theory that has been called – with some hyperbole – "the most famous diagram in social science" ' (Lewinnek, 2010, p.208). Similar models were designed by real estate observers in Paris, where for instance in 1863 the uncle of the famous prefect Baron Haussmann penned a guide to estimating property values based on concentric 'zones' in the capital city. Data composed by realtors proved an invaluable source for early sociologists studying French cities' property dynamics. Maurice Halbwachs's famous 1909 study of Parisian land values drew heavily on the impressive volume of real estate transactions compiled by the real estate agency of John Arthur et Tiffen, published as the *Guide Foncier*, or Land Guide, in 1886.

Halbwachs's volume used real estate prices and transactions as a means to discover patterns and rules of urban growth. While his findings did not embrace the distinct concentric zone model of the Chicago School, he pursued its ideas on the organic nature of the city, concluding that cities develop in accordance with the natural (though perhaps dimly understood) 'needs' of their inhabitants (Topalov, 2006). Back in Chicago, alterations on the concentric model were developed by a realtor, Homer Hoyt, who would become an important contributor to the new discipline of land economics. Hoyt composed his comprehensive *One Hundred Years of Land Values in Chicago* as part of a PhD at the University of Chicago in 1933. This research into land values became the basis for a theory of real estate cycles; his later work with the Federal Housing Administration helped him formulate an

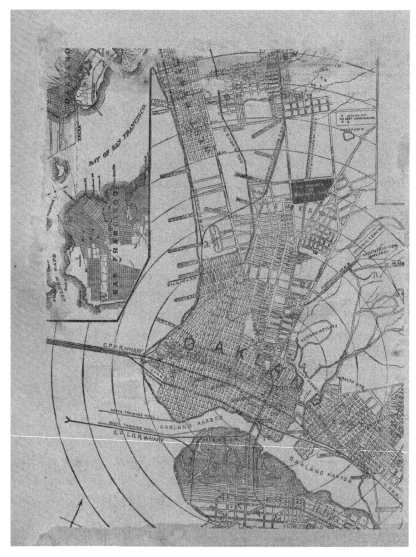

Figure 4 The Roberts And Wolfskill Tract, For Sale by Snyder & Gillis, 467
Ninth Street, Oakland, Cal., United States, 1887.

David Rumsey Map Collection, David Rumsey Map Center, Stanford Libraries.

influential 'sector theory' of urban growth, which revised the concentric
zonal model by suggesting a radial pattern of growth (Beauregard, 2007).[7]

---

[7] Precisely because he was a practising real estate investor and consultant, who had 'planning
concerns' but not 'planning values' (Beauregard, 2007, p.266), Hoyt's work has been side-lined
in the history of planning and urban studies relative to that of his contemporary sociologists.

Real estate, then, provided the substance and background for crucial early work in the social science of urban growth. Yet the economic perspective on urban property and socio-spatial dynamics that it enabled did not become a guiding concern in the field of sociology or urban theory for some time. Classic sociological analyses of the late-nineteenth and early-twentieth century – from Ferdinand Tönnies, Max Weber, and Georg Simmel in Germany, to Louis Wirth and other members of the Chicago School in the United States – remained more concerned with culture, and did not linger over the urban imaginaries and social spaces that real estate could constitute (Davis, 2005). Meanwhile, the international planning movement that coalesced at the turn of the century considered real estate only insofar as property prices circumscribed the sphere of action of public bodies (Ewen and Saunier, 2008; Topalov, 1999). That urban planning enjoyed an important period of inspiration and development in British and French colonial territories, where metropolitan governance ensured that real estate markets did not occupy authoritative positions in urban procedures, potentially accentuated this lack of concern (Demissie, 2009; Home, 2013; King, 1976; Myers, 2003; Wright, 1991).

Still, the cultural life of cities as early urban theory pursued it was fundamentally an inquiry into the operations of cities under capitalism – evidenced in preoccupation with the growth of markets, commoditization, and abstraction and the influence of these forces on human consciousness and community. Critical theorists like Walter Benjamin reflected on the relationship between culture and economy as it informed the landscape and experience of the modern city. Benjamin's *Arcades Project* and his sketches, 'Paris, Capital of the Nineteenth Century (1935/1939)' approached the city as consumerist icon and assemblage, with fragments and ephemera of urban modernity simultaneously moving through and congealing in the built spaces of the city: its department stores, boulevards, theatres, and importantly, commercial arcades. These materials and spaces were expressions of capitalist relations, mediating forces (rather than mere reflections) of their operation; the visual culture of the city both veiled social relations of production (like the commodity, in Marx's formulation) and enabled new kinds of relations and politics to be born. Benjamin's arcades – as he well knew – were speculative real estate ventures, simultaneously a materialization and conduit for capital, as well as for distinct modes of viewing and being in the city (Buck-Morss, 1989; Kingston, 2012; Schwartz, 2001). His valorization of the poet Charles Baudelaire's memorable definition of modernity – 'Modernity is the transient, the fleeting, the contingent; it is one half of art, the other being the eternal and the immovable' – aligns purposively with the fixed and movable components of real estate: the concrete material of built space and land, combined with the circulation of people, goods, and capital it sustains.

As appraisals of capitalism developed in the twentieth century, so, too, did the place accorded to – and instruction taken from – real estate. In the 1970s, in the context of a global surge in land and house prices (Knoll et al., 2014), a political economy approach gained currency in urban studies, and the economistic concerns with real property that had earlier been diverted into land economics and (somewhat less) into urban geography made an influential return to urban theory. Marxist thought provided a central register for this return, and while similar concerns with commoditization and abstraction as had animated critical theorists of urban modernity were important in this move, their more psychological or cultural aspects were downgraded in favour of theorization on regimes of production and labour relations in the making of the city.

Real estate occupies a central role in the thinking of David Harvey, the most important Marxist theorist of cities and urbanization. In *The Limits to Capital* (1982) and elsewhere, Harvey has developed one of the most influential frameworks for reconsidering the role of space in the historical evolution of capitalism. His theory of a 'spatial fix' refers to the ability of capital to reproduce itself and to delay inherent crises of over-accumulation by expanding in space and by circulating through the built environment. Capital is thus 'fixed' – i.e. immobilized – and capitalism itself (temporarily) repaired by redirecting surplus profits from the primary circuit of production and consumption into a secondary circuit of the built landscape. This switching allows the process of accumulation to continue and introduces new temporalities to the process of circulation. The tensions between the speeds at which capital circulates in its different circuits are productive of our built and social spaces. By their very materiality, our cities, factories, homes, and transportation networks enjoy a durability that is at once the condition of their devaluation – capital moves while these spaces do not – and the factor that means that they can constitute a new plane upon which capital will once more reproduce itself after a crisis. In short, the modes through which capital operates are, to Harvey, impossible to grasp without an understanding of the spaces that it appropriates, creates, and in turn, destroys in inevitable crises of devaluation.

Moreover, to summarize more precisely, it is not just *space* that is mobilized by capital's process of reproduction. That the circulation of capital shapes space and place are insights Harvey shares with many urban scholars, most notably French urban theorist Henri Lefebvre (though Harvey claims to have been ignorant of Lefebvre's work at the time of his initial writing.) The mechanism that Harvey finds particularly influential is rental appropriation, which demands the construction of real estate and, importantly, liquid real estate markets.

Capital can take the form of rent (in addition to that of interest or profits) only when 'trade in land is reduced to a special branch of the circulation of interest-bearing capital' – in other words, when land is commoditized and subject to market directives (Harvey, 2018, p.347).

Harvey's insights into the special qualities of real estate as capital and commodity have been deeply influential in urban studies. In John Logan and Harvey Molotch's *Urban Fortunes: The Political Economy of Place* (1987), they undergird 'an effort to construct a sociology of cities on the basis of a sociology of urban property relations' (p.13). Adding a focus on human activism, institution-building, and identity construction to the somewhat anonymous workings of capital privileged in neo-Marxian accounts, their work elaborates on the political and sociological consequences for cities of the tensions between real estate's use and exchange value. Urban 'growth machines', or communities of interest premised on the exploitation of real estate's exchange value, arrange themselves against the 'certain preciousness' that use value represents for owners and residents of particular places – and, indeed, align themselves against growth machines from other cities in an intra-urban competition for capital (Logan and Molotch, 1987, p.17). In this way, the constitutive elements of real estate as a market good produce interest groups of developers, politicians, residents, and community organizers that shape the nature and experience of particular urban places.

In this conceptualization, real estate became a central problematic of studies of neoliberal urbanism. Neoliberal urbanism refers to the way that the restruc-turings associated with the neoliberal turn of the 1980s – particularly, privatiza-tion and market deregulation – operate through and on the urban context. Both the material spaces and governance regimes of cities are transformed as rela-tionships between municipalities, national states, and capital are realigned, in processes that are both global and constitutively uneven (Peck et al., 2009). Restructuring of housing markets is a key terrain for the neoliberalizing process, as public provision of housing is side-lined (sometimes physically destroyed) in favour of market-based, investor-oriented mechanisms of supply. Private devel-opment becomes a privileged agent in an entrepreneurial and competitive international urban system. Gentrification attracted attention early as a key spatial process in neoliberal urbanism. Neil Smith's work explained its patterns with reference to an imagined 'rent gap' between the current returns to a piece of land and the potential returns that would follow from its 'highest and best use' (Smith, 1996, 2002). This gap, the size of which depends on a range of factors – including, as Sharon Zukin (1982) has shown, the place-making and place-branding 'work' of cultural producers and artistic communities – pulls speculative capital in and out of different neighbourhoods as the perceived opportunity for gains increases. In a similar fashion, and as real estate finance is increasingly globalized, capital moves between cities, and contributes significantly to the financialization of the global economy.

Here, theories of neoliberal urbanism dovetail with studies of the 'global city'. Perhaps most familiar thanks to the work of Saskia Sassen (1994), this vein of research aims to re-situate cities – as political entities, sites of economic production, and material assemblages – in studies of globalization. In place of a 'placeless' story of globalization advancing through a spatial flattening born of an ever faster and more frictionless movement of information and capital, the global city literature asserts the significance of the territorialization of global processes at the urban scale. The urban is a place where the global (whatever that is taken to mean) is produced. This perspective, far from relativizing the importance of real estate, reaffirms its status as a central agent in urbanization and the production of urban scales – scales which, as arguments regarding the 'planetary' nature of contemporary urbanization contend, may implicate space far beyond the physical limits of what we experience as cities (Brenner, 2014).[8] Real estate not only composes the crucial sites and material infrastructures necessary for the exchange of things, people, and ideas on a transnational level; it also acts as receptacle and conduit for the capital generated in globalized (and financialized) regimes of production. Harvey's theorization of real estate and capitalism is relevant here: cities – or, more broadly, the urban – are shaped to heighten the efficiency and productivity of capital flows, and the built and social spaces that result (Sassen gives particular attention to the labour market inequalities that characterize global cities) channel and constrain the operation of capital.

3.2 Real Estate and Theories of Urban Futures

In this review, I have reconstructed the place that real estate has occupied in urban theory – an attempt to 'see' urban theory through the lens of real estate. In the process, we can attribute a much deeper historicity to real estate than its deployment in contemporary global city or neoliberal urbanism scholarship implies. This mapping necessarily gives short shrift to important theoretical perspectives on the urban condition that do not attribute overmuch significance to real estate. It is a survey slanted in favour of sociology and geography rather than literary studies or anthropology. And it reproduces a canon, an urban metanarrative, that is in need of revision and qualification. For instance, while

---

[8] Brenner's positions are clarified and contested by responses from Ananya Roy (2016) and contributors to the special issue of *Environment and Planning D: Society and Space* 36(3), 2018, which also includes a response by Brenner.

concerns with race and gender are present throughout this scholarship, they do not enjoy sufficient prominence. Closer attention to intersections of classed 'accumulation by dispossession' with racialized processes of displacement and segregation should be a priority of Marxist urban geography (Wyly et al., 2006). Owing to the way gender shapes the right and ability to own property in capitalist systems, the danger that an urban theory that pivots around real estate narrows our perspective on the city to one of male possession is also potent (Figure 5).

Equally troubling, the location of this theory, which is produced in, for, and about cities of the Global North, is not necessarily up to the challenge of the empirical realities of twenty-first century urbanization, which is overwhelmingly a phenomenon of Latin America, Asia, and Africa. Acknowledging that

Figure 5 Possessive individualism, condo-style. Toronto Man (2019). Sculpture by Stephan Balkenhol for property developers Camrost Felcorp, Toronto, Canada.

Image credit: John Lorinc, used with permission and thanks.

the genealogy traced in this section represents a partial, specifically located view is important. But can we do more? Can real estate serve us as a way of looking that also accords space to marginalized perspectives, that helps to locate new processes and phenomena previously overlooked in the city? And from the other side: are there other turns in urban theory that can help us view and deploy real estate anew?

In her program for a new urban sociology that dispenses with the North/ South, modern/traditional divide, geographer Jenny Robinson suggests that the category of 'ordinary cities', studied and compared through their specific urbanities, can help decentralize concepts of the urban and to reclaim the city from the dominance of transnational flows that seem to inevitably drift outward and downhill from the command-and-control cities of the Global North (Robinson, 2006). A comparative urbanism that will generate claims that are at once more global and more situated – situated in specific places, through specific histories, and in specific knowledge-making paradigms, without suffering exoticization – is necessary to provincialize theory and inform new research on cities worldwide (Chakrabarty, 2000; Sheppard et al., 2015). To the extent that an attention to the material nature of the city can help to re-centre the local spaces in which much of a city's (and citizens') political life transpires, and to bring into focus a necessarily diverse everyday experience of the urban, few objects or processes can accomplish this reorientation and bring us as deeply into the concrete articulation of urban processes as real estate.

The politics of land as it is rendered real estate, often (but not exclusively) at the borderland of the rural and the urban, has proven a rich terrain for both empirical studies and new theorizations of the urban at a global scale. Urban studies scholar Ananya Roy has been at the leading edge of efforts to problematize and reconceptualize the boundary between the formal, official city and the 'unregulated' spaces of slums, shantytowns, or other unofficial settlements (some of them in fact quite wealthy) whose informal land tenure regimes have long been taken as a core feature distinguishing northern from southern urbanization. Rather than view this informality as a residual feature of cities in development, Roy and others have emphasized how 'informal urbanism' is in fact a regime of planning and city-making, shaped from above by state regulation and from below by the everyday practices of urban dwellers (Roy, 2005; Roy and AlSayyad, 2004). (It is also shaped from the side, or in the interstices, by private developers, crime syndicates, and other interest groups (Weinstein, 2008).)

Informality is perhaps the concept that has exhibited the most uptake across the North/South binary, as the discussion in this Element's final section indicates (Hentschel, 2015; Jacquot and Morelle, 2018). In addition to enhancing attention on the daily economic activities and strategies of survival and place-making that transpire outside the formal economy, informality is deeply concerned with struggles over the status of real property ownership, possession, and occupation. It offers a way of revisiting the constitutively unequal processes of making real estate, and emphasizes its 'undecidability' (Roy, 2016). In place of the relatively straightforward 'spatial fix' of global capital, real estate re-emerges as fluid and uncertain, in tune with the 'outside' of capitalist urbanization as it shifts between legal and cultural registers, between mapped and unmapped space, between marketable and unmarketable assets. It also re-emerges as a political artefact, not only defined by state practices but enabling and constraining the political capacities of those it shelters (Appadurai, 2001). In this configuration, real estate serves as a tool to problematize (rather than simply track) the 'uneven geography of spatial value' and resulting subjectivities that mark modern cities (Roy, 2012, p.700; Doshi, 2013).

The dynamics of possession and dispossession through which real estate operates so visibly in theories of capitalist and neoliberal urbanization acquire new depth and extended horizons in scholarship on settler colonialism and the modern city. The settler colonial city occupies a hybrid location in debates on North/South urban theorization. As Blatman-Thomas and Porter (2019) write, such cities are 'displaced': situated in the North, they nevertheless 'embody "South-like" colonial dynamics and are hence neither colonial nor postcolonial'. If urban theory has left the settler-colonial city relatively untouched, even in postcolonial accounts, indigenous studies has also tended to overlook the city and the urban as modes of constructing colonizer-colonized relationships (Porter and Yifchatel, 2019). Yet, recent research suggests that the settler-colonial city represents a particular kind of urban function and process. Settler-colonial urbanism privileges the dispossession of indigenous inhabitants as a constitutive form of urban place-making in imperial societies (Figure 6). This approach centres the racism and violence (intimate, structural, and ongoing) at the heart of defining land as a commodity. When combined with critical indigenous studies, it also centres indigenous resistance and ongoing mobilization to challenge this work of dispossession as part of contemporary urban space (Tomiak, 2017). The unique histories of these cities are one way that a racialized history of capital accumulation, present but rarely foregrounded in critical urban geography, can transform thinking about the production of urban space (Hugill, 2017; Dorries et al., 2019; Blomley, 2014).

As with the fluidity and undecidability of the urban as it emerges from studies of informal urbanism, the built landscape of the settler-colonial city emerges in this theorization as an ongoing terrain of (contested) dispossession, in which property relations serve to de- and re-colonize urban land. These processes

Figure 6 Modern real estate mythologizes its past: Purchase of Manhattan Island by Peter Minuit, 1626, copied from the painting by Alfred Fredericks for the Title Guarantee & Trust Company (c. 1902).

The Miriam and Ira D. Wallach Division of Art, Prints and Photographs: Picture Collection, The New York Public Library Digital Collections. Accessed 7 February 2021. https:// digitalcollections.nypl.org/items/510d47e0-f37f-a3d9-e040-e00a18064a99

develop in concrete terms, as in ever-increasing practices of expulsion and repossession following the 2008 financial crisis (Roy, 2017), as well as in our urban imaginaries, as Lorenzo Veracini (2012) argues in his provocative comparison between suburbanization and settler colonialism. And while land theft is not the only register of oppression and extraction through which settler-colonial societies construct their cities, it is a crucial and foundational one. Thus, as Blatman-Thomas and Porter (2019) suggest, 'analysing how property is performed and materialized reveals the potent work of settler colonialism in the urban context' (p.3).

Following real estate as a technology of imagining and constructing modern cities can thus help globalize urban theory and significantly expand the perspectives brought to bear on urban development. And if the study of real estate pulls the theorist into these conceptual territories, they in turn alter our appreciation for what real estate is capable of, empirically and analytically. They especially offer new appreciation for the racialized processes by which uneven geographies of value are constituted and through which diverse populations are segregated and marginalized. The centrality of local, contextual, and empirical study encouraged by these approaches also requires, as Roy writes, being 'attentive to historical difference as a fundamental constituting process of global political economy', approaching 'the urban as a historical geography, indeed as a historical category' (Roy, 2016, pp.810, 813). Analysing the urban land question in all its complexity is a task that introduces and demands consideration of longer-term political-economic and territorial trajectories. The making and remaking of real estate, with its consequences for the doing and undoing of the urban, pulls urban history into the terrain of theory.

4 The Fleeting and the Fixed: Global Urban Histories of Markets and Land

The purpose of this section is to test out the kind of histories that can result from using real estate as a way of understanding the organization of urban political, economic, and cultural relations. It historicizes real estate, offering accounts of moments and places in which the assemblage of modern real estate markets and urban property relations are particularly visible and consequential. These are not exhaustive accounts of real estate enterprise or rental relations or property rights (etc., etc.) in any given locale. Rather, each section assembles experiences from different cities, using real estate as a way of pulling seemingly disparate environments into a shared narrative and analytic frame. In the first section, real estate is approached as a mode of circulation via an examination of the historical specificity of what we now call, without much reflection, the modern real estate market. Starting from changes in regimes of production and accumulation in the nineteenth century, this section tracks a new disposition toward real estate on the part of investors, owners, consumers, and users. This disposition connects the experiences of urban development and experience across diverse cities, and also reveals new actors and impulses at work in global movements of capital. In the second section, the foregrounding of real estate's 'real' and fixed elements, especially land, illuminates historically specific processes of making urban property and its attendant politics. In pursuing real estate in two broad modalities, these sections present historical accounts of the organization of urban relations rooted in particular times and places that, while emphasizing commonalities and transfers, also suggest ways of posing comparative questions of other contexts.

These divisions map broadly onto the double life of real estate in market societies: its capacity for mobilization (of capital, people, and things) and its reliance on fixity (of capital in buildings and land; of buildings and land in space; of people in jurisdictions) (Yates, 2019b). The management of this double life is the basic remit of property rights, assembled through legal mechanisms and institutions – from the contract to the corporation to the trust – with an eye to ordering claims, assuring value, and allocating risk. These rights are also assembled so as to govern cities and populations, elaborating durable infrastructures that can fix, channel, and manage the mobile and fragile lives of urban inhabitants (Chhabria, 2019).

As these sections will show, pulling this double life apart is somewhat artificial. Consider, for example, one important property institution, the *waqf*: an Islamic pious endowment commonly based upon real estate assets, used widely across the Muslim world. Waqf is an example of both the contingent and enduring nature of these tensions between movement and fixity. Often viewed as an immobilization of capital – and consequently an obstacle to economic modernization – waqf has been revised in recent scholarship to highlight the way that its arrangement of property claims remained imbricated in market relations. As agents in urban space, a waqf contributed to local economies by providing spaces for public institutions and social reproduction, like schools, hospitals, religious buildings, and markets; they generated revenues through layers of leasing and subletting – trafficking in use rights – with tenants entitled to ownership of premises they constructed. They stretched these relations across scales, helping to cement an individual's property and status in a local context while also funding activities abroad, such as pilgrim support in distant holy cities. In the view of historian Pascale Ghazaleh, a waqf isolated certain goods from the 'default setting of potentially anonymous market transactions', but did not prevent their commercialization; indeed, by fostering communities of interest around real estate and its income, endowments could arrange and introduce market relations where they were previously absent (Ghazaleh, 2017, p.114; Beverley, 2018). This is not to say that they are no more than common-law trusts in another guise, camouflaging a fundamentally capitalist orientation to patrimony. Rather, it is to point out that the legal and cultural work of aligning real estate's alienability and its embeddedness is foundational to its operations, and that parsing this complexity – the experiment the following sections undertake – offers ways of pursuing meaningful comparative analysis of property relations and the cities they shape.

4.1 Mobilizing Real Estate: Markets for the Modern City

Real estate markets so dominate popular and policy discourse on the contemporary city that it is hard to imagine cities without them. Certainly, the basics of real estate market activity – building, renting, buying, selling urban property – have long (perhaps always) been carried on in cities (Béguin and Lyon-Caen, 2018; Casson and Casson, 2016; Chauvard, 2005; Harding, 2002). And yet, for these operations and transactions to coalesce into something called a 'market', stocked with commodities and shepherded by specialized intermediaries – especially a market that is perceived to be a powerful, even dominant force in the urban environment –' is historically specific. From the mid-nineteenth century, modern cities have undertaken a marked evolution, from a time when real estate provided a stable backdrop for urbanity to one when the economic development of real estate became a core function of the metropolis, even a driver of the national and international economy. In what follows, we pursue this emergence of a market mode for real estate across multiple scales, from structural transformations in the global economy that changed the financial role of real estate, to the ramifications of these changes on owners, traffickers, and users of urban real estate, all of which combined to valorize – at significant social cost – property's market relations.

Informed observers and ordinary people alike could recognize that something new was happening with urban real estate toward the end of the nineteenth century. Journals of record communicating real estate transactions to an interested public appeared in 1858 in England with the publication of the *Estates Gazette* and from 1868 with New York City's *Real Estate Record and Builders' Guide*. In 1868, the restoration of the Meiji dynasty in Japan inaugurated a new treatment of real property, as land was transformed into a tradable good, with distinct consequences for the transformation of Edo – now Tokyo – into a renovated capital (Hein, 2010). In Mexico City, the expropriation of urban church and indigenous property from the 1850s 'created a new market for urban real estate', which the Porfirian government fostered through land sales to investors and speculators in the 1870s and 1880s (Lear, 1996, p.459). In Atlanta, real estate developers numbered only six in the city's directory in 1867 but exploded to fifty-five by 1891 (Lands, 2002, p.550). Looking around at a building boom transforming Paris in the early 1880s, a French parliamentary commission reported that, 'the modern building sector is less industry than it is commerce; transactions are constant, eradicating production, in a manner of speaking'. Indeed, it concluded, 'for the public at large, the building entrepreneur is a merchant, almost a broker, just like the head of a department store' (Procès-verbaux, 1884, p.1619). In Manhattan, the Real Estate Exchange and Auction Room was opened in 1885, replacing an older Real Estate Exchange Salesroom and organizing real estate brokers on a new footing. Lyon incorporated a central auction house for real estate in 1880, Boston in 1889, Charleston in 1907.

Structural changes in the global economy laid the foundations for these synchronous developments. As the competitive impulses unleashed by the industrialized growth of the first two thirds of the nineteenth century led to progressively diminished returns on capital, a search for alternative outlets gave real estate – particularly housing – a more significant role as a mode of accumulation. Merchant investment in urban land increased dramatically in Bombay from the 1870s, while in Rio de Janeiro the shift from a mercantile and slave-based economic regime in the late-nineteenth century also channelled local capital into urban real estate, especially rental housing, aided by legal reforms from 1850 that effectively created private property in Brazil for the first time (Ribeiro, 1989). The great depression that afflicted advanced capitalist economies in Europe and the United States between the 1870s and 1890s saw declining wages and rising unemployment for workers, but ramped up returns on profits invested via the expanding institutions and networks of global finance (Arrighi, 2010). The result was a global frontier in real estate development and financialization. In Britain, agricultural depression spurred legal reforms that liberalized land transfers in England (the Settled Land Act of 1882) while enhancing the appeal of investment in farms, ranches, and other productive landed developments abroad. 1885–1913 saw a boom in tradable companies with foreign land transactions on the London Exchange, from 200 to more than 1,500 (Christopher, 1985). The perceived stability and prestige of real estate aligned with the self-image and saving traditions of both large and small retail investors – moreover, as Paige Glotzer shows, the willingness of companies funnelling investment capital from Britain to US urban real estate to enforce racial segregation and link white ownership to profitability further boosted the popularity of such investments (Glotzer, 2020). But at the same time, a potentially greater transformation occurred as real estate abroad was configured and taken up as a pure financial asset, with little concern for its use or material nature. The consolidation of landed private property in Egypt in 1891, intended to secure and satisfy peasants threatened by the large plantations of the region's cotton-exporting classes, facilitated foreign investment that moved swiftly from rural to urban lands, shifting from loans for farming to investments in mortgage insurance and urban development schemes (Jakes, 2020) (Figures 7 and 8). Local circumstances stimulating real estate speculation – such as the founding of a republic in Brazil in 1889, the completion of the Dakar–Saint-Louis railway in Senegal in 1885, or the announcement of the arrival of a Canadian Pacific rail line in Winnipeg in 1881 – were situated instantiations of national and transnational stories of redirected flows of capital.

This wave of financialization took advantage of changes in the treatment and circulation of real property that began earlier in the century and which are best

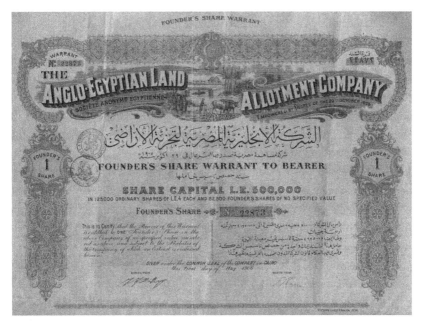

Figures 7 and 8 Securities representing international investment in Egyptian land from the early twentieth century.

Aaron Jakes, used with permission and thanks.

captured under the rubric of commercialization. In England from the 1840s, as historian Desmond Fitz-Gibbon argues, debates and projects for the reform of real property registration and circulation demonstrated a 'new commercial discourse shaping public understandings of real estate' (Fitz-Gibbon, 2018, p.129). Comparison and analogy between real property and personal property – between real property and commercial merchandise – became axiomatic in those circles of legal and political economic discussion in which the marketization of real property was fiercely contested. This was a constitutively transnational debate, whose terms and projects travelled with remarkable consistency across national boundaries. John Stuart Mill's contention, in his *Principles of Political Economy* (1848), that 'to make land as easily transferable as stock would be one of the greatest economical improvements which could be bestowed on a country', emerges nearly verbatim from the pens of real estate company boosters in France, who wooed investors by explaining that 'making land, its constructions, and its revenues, into paper titles that are folded and placed in a wallet, that pass from hand to hand, is the final word in progress', and from land reformers in Algeria who assured readers that 'the day an Arab can bring his property title to the state pawnshop or sell it on the market, like he sells a load of wheat, won't that be of profit to Europeans?' (Fitz-Gibbon, 2018, p.130; Bailleux de Marisy, 1881, p.444; Guyot, 1885, p.204). Criticisms were similarly mimetic. Fitz-Gibbon cites barrister J. M. Ludlow, who, in an 1859 presentation, warned that, 'I can conceive of no more frightful and anti-social state of things, than ... that in which every estate in England could be daily quoted at the Stock Exchange', while courts consulted on the desirability of enhanced land transfers in France expressed identical dread at the prospect of 'family farms spread out on the gaming table, mixed in with bearer bonds in the corridors of the Stock Exchange' (*Documents*, 1844, vol.1, p.553). Anxiety to defend the territorial patrimony of consolidating nation-states from the market was evident in legislative moves to protect smallholders from dispossession, as in homesteading laws passed in France in the 1890s (modelled on measures in the United States), and new laws against 'alien' land ownership in the United States Midwest (McFarlane, 1987).

In cities, ambivalence regarding the commercialization of real estate was less potent, but still consequential. A liberal, private model of the city, characterized by an understanding of urban real estate as a privately held good dictating urban development, was essentially inviolable in Europe, North America, and much colonized territory until the Great War. Certainly, it faced well-known challenges by century's end. An increasingly assertive transatlantic municipal movement gave traction to the progressive notion of public management of urban amenities, and housing reformers gained some limitations on the autonomy of private proprietorship through hygienic regulation (Ewen and Saunier, 2008; Rodgers, 1998). In imperial settings, where the privileges of private property ownership enjoyed less stability and more constrained authority over urban development, emergencies like the third bubonic plague outbreak at the turn of the century stimulated still more extensive public interventions on private prerogatives (Bigon, 2016; Echenberg, 2010). Yet even here, the logic of a property market was absorbed and appropriated rather than suppressed. The case of the Bombay Improvement Trust, formed in 1898, gives a sense of how this worked. In response to the plague outbreak, the Trust initiated an aggressive campaign of slum clearance and building regulation, over the fierce opposition of local property owners and landlords. The process saw the Trust become an important urban property owner in its own right, concerned with improving the values and returns of its own portfolio (Hazareesingh, 2001; Issar, 2017). Measures to municipalize real estate and direct its development to public ends thus reinforced rather than undermined its status as a commercial object. As Prashant Kidambi (2007) shows, the Trust's valuations to determine compensation for expropriated landlords, for instance, were carried out on the basis of hypothetical development possibilities, as owners of little-built lots argued that they were owed indemnities that recognized potential 'highest and best use' of the land in the future. Over time and through contestation, the acknowledgement of future, speculative returns as a key aspect of land's valuation became routine in legal rulings (Tejani, 2020). Public movements to subjugate urban real estate's market relations certainly had important outcomes, but made few successful dents in the authority and jurisdiction of private property.

An embrace of commoditized property in fact became an arrow in the quiver of urban real estate owners as they defended their interests. In Bombay as in other large cities in Europe and North America, urban property responded to threats of municipalization and de-marketization by organizing, taking instruction from the range of economic interests, large and small, that increasingly drew livings and profits from urban real estate. In Germany and France, urban property owners mobilized by claiming to 'run property ownership on a business basis' – in other words, to be engaged in an entrepreneurial endeavour that placed them within the useful, dynamic classes of the commercial economy (Forsell, 2006, p.85; Michel, 2006). Property owners were job-makers, as their organized representatives in Stockholm argued in the early twentieth century, employing myriad trades and professionals to maintain their buildings. They were also service-providers (an argument commonly used in Berlin and Paris), supplying urban residents with shelter and associated services. Defending the privatized city, these groups added a discourse of commercial enterprise – of market making – to more traditional, liberal arguments in favour of the utility and significance of private property (Yates, 2015, Chapter 3).

Several important trends illuminate the impact of real estate's commercialization. The first was a transformation in the distribution of real estate capital in nineteenth-century metropoles. Large cities, competing with and copying one another in their modernization schemes, displayed a marked 'embourgeoisement' of property ownership, with rising real estate values increasingly captured by urban elites. In Rio de Janeiro, for instance, Zephyr Frank's studies of the urban property market between the 1840s and 1880s show an increasing concentration of real estate fortunes among the highest classes in the city, accompanied by a proliferation of smallholdings among the more modest orders – in other words, increasing inequality in real estate capital even as absolute rates of ownership registered less significant changes (Frank, 2018). In Paris, a similar trend seems to hold, in that urban property owners belonged increasingly to the higher classes by the time of the Great War, though ownership itself was not dramatically more concentrated (Daumard, 1965; Choko, 1997). The release of land from Church and indigenous holdings in Mexico City from mid-century – an amount that totalled nearly 50 per cent of the city's surface – led to its concentration in the hands of 'a new landed elite' (Morales, 1975). Frequently enjoying close ties to Europe and America, these owners undertook developments that emulated the monumental metropolitan and class-specific residential forms of Europe, defining Mexico City 'as a modern, urbane environment in which international entrepreneurs and investors could operate in comfort and even luxury' (Reese, 2002, p.143; Sheinbaum, 2010). Finally, in Bombay, by 1910 almost half of the city's land – the other half chiefly controlled by the government and its municipal corporation – belonged to about five hundred powerful landlords (Hazareesingh, 2000). There were important exceptions and countervailing trends to these developments; the working-class self-building that characterized urban expansion in the growing cities of North America was a notable check on landlordism, while the lower middle classes in Europe remained attached to small ownership (Choko and Harris, 1990; Crossick, 2000; Green and Owens, 2013). Yet on the whole, the changes in urban proprietorship and to property's role in national political economies were in favour of concentration

A second trend was a transformation in the amount and direction of corporate capital in urban property markets. The corporate property owner was not strictly speaking a new element of urban real estate in the nineteenth century. Collective institutions – from churches, hospitals, and universities to guilds, *awqāf*, and imperial trading companies – were influential forces in the built and urban landscape globally from the early modern period. In Edinburgh, as Richard

Rodger shows, trusts were key players in urban real estate from the seventeenth century onwards; by the nineteenth, institutional owners constituted over two-fifths of landowners with holdings larger than one acre (Rodger, 2002, pp.7–8). The slow and durable quality of these entities' operations, designed to produce steady and reliable returns over the long run, often entailed little that distinguished them from 'traditional' individual property owners for whom security and patrimony were overwhelming concerns. But the nature of collective ownership changed over the nineteenth century. The growth of trusts and of enterprises such as insurance companies and savings banks that were required by law to place their funds in stable investments translated into an increase in both corporate financing and ownership of urban real estate (Blackmar, 2005, 2013; Yates, 2015) (Figure 9).[9] And the rise of speculative companies on the limited-liability model, oriented to generating profits for shareholders from urban real estate, marked an influential new attitude toward property management (Bonneval and Robert, 2019; Lescure, 1980). As the annual report of one Parisian property investment firm, the Compagnie Foncière de France (founded 1879) explained succinctly to shareholders: '[the company's] top priority is obtaining the highest possible returns from its real estate portfolio'.[10] Even though such ownership was far from dominant in quantitative terms, it had outsized effects on the norms and discourses surrounding property development. The invocation of urban real estate's 'business basis' by organized property owners, touched on above, is one indication of shifting attitudes; another is the spread of professional property intermediaries, discussed below, that fit (and exploited) this developing market ethos around real estate.

The consequences of these changes were weighty because of a third critical trend: the assimilation of urban real estate to the increasingly politicized issue of housing. At the turn of the century, most city dwellers were tenants – even many owners rented – and the dominant economic relationship mediated by real estate capital was the landlord-tenant relation.[11] This relationship was also the locus of contentious politics; the rent issue was a fierce transnational debate at century's end, and migrated from the countryside to the city in the writings of activists like Henry George or the reform ambitions of progressives like Octavia Hill (Guldi, 2018). The decades leading to the Great War

---

[9] These funds also spread their capital and transformed property relations beyond the city; see Maggor, 2017, and Levy, 2013.

[10] Archives Nationales du Monde du Travail, 65 AQ I 102: Compte Rendu présenté au nom du conseil d'administration de la Compagnie Foncière de France, par M. Sauret, président. Exercice 1884, pp.13–15.

[11] The global rise of owner-occupancy following the Second World War cemented the cultural association of property ownership with housing, but marked a significant transformation in the role of real estate capital in social reproduction and urban politics.

Figure 9 Corporate cityscapes: plaque on a pre-war Parisian apartment building
indicating ownership by the insurance company L'Abeille.
Photo by author.

was a period of intense housing crisis globally. In British India, urban rents
rose at a dramatic rate, particularly in Karachi, Bombay, Madras, Rangoon,
and Calcutta (Bhattacharyya, 2018). In Paris, tenants mobilized against rising
rents in the real estate boom of the 1880s, coinciding with well-publicized
eviction crises in rural Ireland. Parisian renters formed official organizations
in the 1910s, taking a leading role in widespread consumer protests against *la
vie chère* or the high price of living (Magri, 1996; Shapiro, 1985) (Figure 10).
Rent strikes hit Barcelona in 1905, Buenos Aires and New York in 1907, and
Glasgow in 1915; organizing continued throughout the war, achieving rent
control regulation in large cities around the world in the post-war period
(Baer, 1993; Englander, 1983; Fogelson, 2013; Gray, 2018). The business
basis of real estate, then, intersected in complex ways with a growing

Figure 10 Tenant organization: a public relocation orchestrated by Georges Cochon and the Parisian Tenants' Union, c. 1926. The group (founded 1911) staged interventions to remove tenants threatened with expulsions and property seizures and to otherwise thwart landlords.

Bibliothèque Nationale de France.

conscience of housing as a right: it created the difficult material conditions that birthed the 'housing question' while also providing the commercial imaginary through which housing could be rolled into the burgeoning consumer rights' struggles of the early twentieth century (Stovall, 2012).

This was the first age of global real estate: longer-term changes in the legal and cultural imaginary of real property helped prepare the ground for a massive reorientation of global capital near the end of the nineteenth century that saw real estate playing a key role in the global financialization of capital at the turn of the twentieth century. Large cities around the world evidenced shifts in the distribution of real estate capital, the increasing presence of for-profit corporations as owners and managers of urban real estate, and the rise of a new discourse of housing rights, all of which contributed to placing urban real estate production on a more homogenous market footing.

On the level of the everyday during this worldwide reorientation, there was much in the formation and use of the urban fabric that remained unchanged. The 'shelter business', as Michael Doucet and John Weaver observe, 'continued to develop property in the traditional way', engaging 'a small and constant cast of actors including landowners, sub-dividers, lawyers, registry officers, builders, tradesmen and laborers, municipal officials, and real estate or land agents' (Doucet and Weaver, 1984, p.234). The local scale – both nearby places and close-knit information networks – remained intensely relevant to development. In his work on nineteenth-century Rio de Janeiro, for example, Frank suggests that networks of property owners and their information exchanges were more responsible for shifts in property value than geography per se: 'It is as if these blocks "knew" more about what went on in other blocks, owing to the way that the owners connected them across the city.' (Frank, 2018, p.557). Nevertheless, the recognizably modern property markets that emerged in these cities represented significant changes in the dispositions and designs of their principal agents, even where and if some production processes demonstrated continuity with 'traditional' methods (Harris, 2012; Karr, 2015). As the commoditization of urban land became a truly global affair, small- and medium-scale operators exhibited similar development practices, particularly on the peripheries of large cities, where they tracked extending avenues, utilities, and urban rail lines and acquired land, subdividing and reselling lots surrounding Rio de Janeiro, Mexico City, Paris, Bombay, and Boston (Figures 11 and 12). Regulatory contexts, financial networks, architectural form, and eventual residents could be different in each instance, but speculative suburban developments from the 1860s participated in a globalized trafficking of what historian Jordan Sand, writing on suburban development in Tokyo, labels 'fantasy images' of more peaceful, salubrious, and fashionable urban living (Sand, 2005, p.136).

These images were the wares of a new kind of specialized intermediary: the real estate agent, the icon and underwriter of the new property market. The occupation initially encapsulated a range of intermediaries but was increasingly standardized by the turn of the twentieth century; its practitioners constituted 'the flesh and blood behind the distilled statements of land-use theory', occupying 'an important social position mediating between a bourgeoisie with funds to invest and tenants residing in the investment dwellings' (Doucet and Weaver, 1984, p.235). Their activities were a formative component of urbanization and important to the shaping of a modern urban culture, one premised upon the flux of valorized city milieus, the circulation of residential space, and its transformation into a distinct asset class. In cities of the United States, Western Europe, East Asia, and Europe's colonial territories – anywhere the global bourgeoisie found purchase – they developed and exploited urban phenomena that became key elements of the commercialized approach to urban real estate: the rise of popular journalism (from the spread of mass newspapers to the intensification of commercial advertising and exhibitions); the growth of tourism; and the spread

Figure 11 Fashionable living in French suburbs: a poster advertising lots for sale in the environs of Paris, c. 1900.

Archives Départementales des Hauts-de-Seine.

of white-collar employment (including, importantly, the country-spanning peregrinations of rotating rosters of staff of imperial bureaucracies).

In North America, as Jeffrey Hornstein (2005) chronicles, agents began coordinating in local real estate boards from 1875, beginning in the booming West and Midwest and reaching most large and middling cities by 1910. Brokers modelled these boards on stock exchanges that coordinated the sale of securities. They instituted rules for membership and harmonized sales practices, creating standard lease forms and commission schedules and

Figure 12 Escaping industrial Pittsburgh: 'University Park where 300 residence sites invite the home builder-the investor; The wonderful sale is now on! An event in Allegheny's history', 1895.

Library of Congress.

collecting data on properties, in addition to setting times and places for buyers and sellers (or their representatives) to meet. By working to make transactions more efficient – all with a supposed eye to improving the satisfaction of the client – real estate boards were also aiming to moralize the field, replacing a free-for-all of rogue agents with a professional brotherhood of responsible intermediaries. Improving the image of the real estate broker, the thinking went, would be a boon for business, as expunging disreputable figures who might discredit the field would reduce competition as well as garner a larger clientele reassured by the perceived trustworthiness of the remaining professionals. (Indeed, this professional brotherhood was only slowly opened to women and brokers of colour – marginalized people for whom real estate's low barriers to entry offered an important means of social mobility, but whom the professional movement in the field deliberately excluded (Figure 13). The segregated nature of American cities and housing finance in fact created distinct organizations for African American professionals.) Boards joined in a national association just before the Great War, and by the 1920s, agents had obtained the holy grail of professionalization:

112   SIMMS' BLUE BOOK AND DIRECTORY

ILLINOIS

H. A. Watkins was born in Pulaski County, Illinois in 1883; worked on farm until 1904; lived in Decatur, Illinois 1913, 1914; came to Chicago November, 1914; went into the real estate business on July 15, 1915, was successful and is one of the largest real estate operators of our Race in the City of Chicago; owns and pays taxes on over $100,000 worth of real estate.

Mr. Watkins married Anna M. Leverett of Hopkinsville, Kentucky in 1910 and resides in a beautiful $20,000 resi-

MR. H. A. WATKINS
Office 3510 Indiana Ave.
Douglas 1714

dence at 3657 Michigan Ave. He is a member of the Metropolitan Community Center, the Peoples Church; one of the directors and treasurer of the Metropolitan Community Center, is chairman of the Metropolitan Sunday Evening Club; member of the board of directors of the Pyramid Building & Loan Association; member of the Board of Management of the Wabash Branch of the Y. M. C. A., Vice-President of the Board and Chairman of the Committee of Finance; is a member of the Executive Committee of the Salvation Army; he is a member of the Appomattox Club; is a 32nd degree Mason; member of the Arabic Temple No. 44; Member of the Improved Benevolent Protective Order of Elks of the World, Knights of Pythias, Odd Fellows, Mosaic Temple of America, Knights and Daughters of Africa.

Residence
MR. AND MRS. WATKINS
3657 Michigan Ave.

Figure 13 The entry for H. A. Watkins, real estate and insurance man, in J. N. Simms's *Blue Book and National Negro Business and Professional Directory* (Chicago, 1923).

Schomburg Center for Research in Black Culture, Jean Blackwell Hutson Research and Reference Division, The New York Public Library, Digital Collections. Accessed 8 February 2021. https://digitalcollections.nypl.org/items/510d47df-759e-a3d9-e040-e00a18064a99

ILLINOIS

REAL ESTATE AND INSURANCE

Mortgage Loans, Deals Financed. We Write Insurance, Fire, Theft, Bombing and Explosion, Automobile, Plate Glass, Compensation and Public Liability.

Figure 13 Cont.

state licensing, which enforced barriers to entry and standards of practice. Along the way, the influence of boards on their local real estate markets was profound. Despite representing a small minority of active brokers, the rules and habits of transactions they established – as well as the data on real estate they collected – set the terms for property exchange in their localities.

Realtors in the United States were more than brokers specialized in real property, and their activities demonstrate that the labour of market making was cultural as much as it was economic or structural. For Hornstein, these new commercial professionals embodied a particular middle-class culture, bound up in the moral task of property ownership and a 'market masculinity' of commercial mastery and entrepreneurial endeavour (even as their clients were increasingly white-collar professionals and 'organization men' rather than independent businessmen). The turn-of-the-century professionalization of their occupation was a kind of coming to terms with the new business of space represented by the closing of the frontier and the new vocational identities represented by urbanization: 'dealing in land, in space, in providing places for those on the move, the broker's essential function brought together the migrant and the hearthstone. Two sets of ostensibly antagonistic tendencies at the heart of American culture – mobility and stability, business and the professions – met in the figure of the real estate man' (Hornstein, 2005, p.5) (Figure 14).

Realtors did not play this precise cultural role in any other national setting; indeed, the term itself is a trademarked designation for US brokers. Yet the North American model was (and remains) seductive for brokers elsewhere, though its application has been uneven. Studying the politics of property in interwar Britain, Avner Offer (1981) observes that the market transparency brought about and valorized by the *Estates Gazette* and the operations of the Auction Mart in London before the Great War were reversed in the 1920s, as new informational monopolies were formed and property intermediation reoriented around exclusivity. Estate agents and auctioneers in the United Kingdom achieved statutory registration only in 1979, though they still are not subject to licensing requirements (Latham, 2017). In France, estate agents founded their first national occupational associations in the interwar period, but did not succeed in achieving licensing and professional charter until 1970 (Yates, 2012). These different national trajectories are indications of diverging cultures of property and possession in the twentieth century – themselves reflective of distinct political economies of real estate, and suggestive of the utility of pursuing the intermediary as an entry point into comparing these processes and understanding their implications.

The agents, trends, and practices that converged from the second half of the nineteenth century to establish real estate markets as arbiters of urban property, housing, and development created resilient modes of imagining and constructing modern cities. Over considerable periods of time and dramatic transformations – most notably, the interjection of government-supplied and regulated urban housing on a world-wide scale following the Second World War – this market mode has demonstrated the capacity to withstand the contradictions and oppositions thrown up by its own operations. Of course, the market mode is not evenly distributed in time or space, and it is never uncontested. As the scholarship on the socialist city touched on above suggests, the making and unmaking of real estate markets is frequently recapitulated in the modern era (Marcuse, 1996; Verdery, 2003). The case for marketized provision of housing is restated everywhere it faces efforts to curb its jurisdiction. For examples, we can turn to the lobbying efforts in 1970s France that persuasively made the case for a return to individual, owner-occupied housing after years of successful public provision of mass housing (Mulvey, 2016), or to contemporary Cairo, where a so-called 'new rental law' introduced in 1996 aims to free a housing market

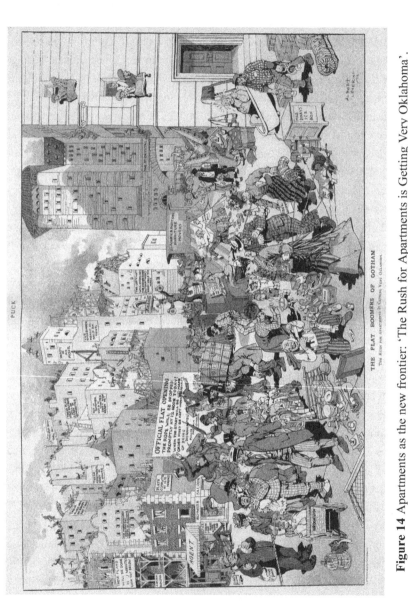

Figure 14 Apartments as the new frontier: 'The Rush for Apartments is Getting Very Oklahoma'.

Albert Levering, The Flat Boomers of Gotham, *Puck*, 1906. Library of Congress.

'captured' by the state since the imposition of rental controls in 1947 (El-Kazaz, 2018; Shawkat, 2020). Indeed, the market model has underlaid and been imbricated throughout even state provision initiatives, as public-private partnerships in the UK and elsewhere demonstrate (Shapely, 2013). Because real estate operates through differentiating spaces and populations of value, it is constitutively uneven and unstable, thriving on the greater profits to be enjoyed at the disjunctures and thresholds of accumulation (Cavalcanti, 2014).

The endurance and irrepressibility of real estate's markets are in part explained by the significance of their contributions to modern urban cultures. The business of real estate is a traffic in ideas of the city, of modernity, of the self, as much as it is a commerce in land and buildings (Searle, 2016). The circulation of these imaginaries means real estate is as important to urban culture as it is to urban land use. There are very plain ways that this is seen to be true, as in the marketing activities of agents that communicate ideals and fantasies of urban living. But reflection on the particularity of real estate as a commodity suggests more complex tasks of cultural mediation as well, particularly with regards to temporalities of the urban. Speculative development, which dominates real estate production today, is an act of projecting. Aiming at a specific future, it normalizes – because it requires – the idea of urban growth and delineates a direction of travel for the city. In practical terms, the business hinges upon timing, riding a cycle of booms and busts as the clock counts down on financing, while the real estate package holds different temporalities within itself: the pre-existing and long-lasting qualities of land, the durable nature of built structures – and, in contrast, the fluctuating and temporary nature of some constructions and some territories. Durability in the face of uncertain futures is of course one way that real estate makes itself difficult to reckon with in the urban environment, as anyone who has lived near a brownfield or abandoned factory can attest. Projecting is a means by which real estate reinforces the forward-looking obsession of (capitalist) market culture. Jarring disjunctures and overlaps between past, present, and future, between the durable and the fleeting, are operationalized in and through real estate, and contribute to the complex structures of feeling – the mental life of the metropolis – governing the modern urban experience.

4.2 Fixing Real Estate: Property in the Modern City

Turning land into real estate is premised on the construction of private property and on the integration of that property into circuits of economic production, in which it operates especially as a store of capital and a generator of value based on its exchangeability. Property enacts takings and enclosures, often glossed as 'accumulation by dispossession', which this Element has placed at the heart of the definition of real estate. It was a central project of modern empires and their stakeholders, for whom the implementation and rationalization of property rights advanced profitability, jurisdiction, and sovereignty (Banner, 2007; Greer, 2018; Herzog, 2015; Weaver, 2003). Dates and statutes representing the establishment of commoditized private property pepper this volume: the 1850 Land Law in Brazil (effective from 1854); the 1858 Ottoman Land Code; 1891 decrees regularizing most private property in land in Egypt. To these we can add the 1793 'rule of property' embedded in the Permanent Settlement of Britain's Indian jurisdictions, the French Revolution's enshrining of absolute private property rights in 1789 (reinforced by laws on registration in 1855), and the proliferation of title registration laws that followed the example of the Australian Torrens System (1858): from land reform in Tunisia in 1885, to Korean registration laws in 1910, to laws passed by the Second Parliament in Iran in 1911, to name only a few (Blaufarb, 2016; Chehabi, 2019; Guha, 1963; Isamoglu, 2004; Maier, 2016). This global story of private property in land has a distinctly and importantly urban element. As urban geographers Richard Harris and Ute Lehrer (2018) stress in their survey of the suburban land question, property mechanisms have particularly crucial functions and consequences in the urban context. Thanks to the city's density and changeability – the 'restless urban landscape' (Knox, 1991) – property there is particularly policed, monitored for encroachments or digressions, and scrutinized for political and economic opportunity. Urban sites 'were the places where land first became a commodity, where the land market was first, and most closely, regulated and where it now frames the future' (Harris and Lehrer, 2018, p.24).

This rush of competitive and emulative legislation throughout the nineteenth century was by no means the last word on the commoditization of land, urban or otherwise. (Indeed, in many contexts, it was not the *first* word, as research on the history of customary land designations and marketability demonstrates (Brady, 2018).) These legal codes sanctifying individualized private property were not as totalizing as is frequently assumed; multiple forms of land tenure persist even in the most heavily marketized and neoliberalized settings, and in colonial contexts, overlapping and parallel systems of property were often the rule. For instance, in Lagos following British annexation in 1861, individual property became newly accessible (with particular consequences for some slaves and former slaves, for whom ownership represented special autonomy in the local social order) but family ownership persisted – indeed, Crown grants and other fee-simple titles often reverted to this older form of tenure and remained tolerated by British courts (Hopkins, 1980; Mann, 2007). The law, which plays a powerful role in Western countries in codifying the reproduction of capital, can resurrect alternative modes of possession and endow them with the protected qualities of private property – witness the victory of Maya land right claims based on collective use in Belize in 2007 (shaped, in fact, by the Supreme Court's invocation of a Privy Council decision based on a Nigerian land dispute from the 1920s) (Pistor, 2019). Moreover, land itself 'remembers'; the distinct historical conditions that shape land's distribution before newer, more homogenized systems of ownership are implemented can create institutional, discursive, and material imprints that shape its later operations (Peñalver, 2008–2009, 2011). Meanings associated with particular sites, such as shrines or sites of burial, can perpetuate decades of negotiation that effectively shift such spaces between domains of public and private property, marketable and demarketized land. (To demonstrate the point quite materially, consider the efforts of British authorities in colonial Accra to halt the local practice of burying family members in the earthen floors of houses, as a condition of facilitating urban property sales (Balakrishnan, 2019).) Common feelings of ownership can diverge from statutory definitions of property and proprietorship and remain supported (or at least uncontested) by authorities, and validated by other forms of legitimation, sometimes for considerable stretches of time.

This section considers material components of the propertied city, land and buildings, surveying recent work that examines the history of particular cities from – literally – the ground up. It privileges the materiality of property as an entry point into the specificity of place, and looks at two principal settings – cities in India and in Brazil – to demonstrate how new kinds of urban histories can emerge from this approach. This geographical focus is dictated by the state of current research, which is shaped by several trends, foremost among them an interest in informality as a defining feature of contemporary, especially postcolonial, urbanization. Informality grants a particular importance to the examination and stakes of land use transformation, especially at the urban fringes, where scholars from urban ecologists to critical geographers have developed a host of labels to attempt to analyse the 'edges' and 'peripheries' of urbanization and urban belonging (Angelo, 2017; Tzaninis et al., 2021). If we want to study changes in urban property regimes, then, these are the places and this is the scholarship that stand to most immediately inform our understanding.

The urban question is in fundamental ways a land question. As historian Mariam Dossal writes in her study of modern Mumbai, when it comes to cities, 'the *land question dominates all others*' (Dossal, 2010, p.xxix; emphasis original). Yet Dossal's urban history is uncharacteristic in framing its account so directly around the politics of land use. Typically, land figures in urban history principally as a geographical condition shaping a city's morphology. The swamps that require filling (and whose subsequent seasonal flooding reduce land values and determine which communities might have access to them); the hills that constrain development and shelter squatters; the granite bedrock that surfaces and supports skyscrapers – these are natural features that human settlement must negotiate, the 'landscape' that frequently slips from the urban historian's view once the first street is plotted. This neglect is lessened in works of urban environmental history, where 'natural' and 'built' landscapes interact as agents in urbanization. In William Cronon's influential study of Chicago as 'Nature's Metropolis', for instance, a string of narrative devices remind the reader of the persistent interdependence of the human and the natural – from the very title of the work, to hybrid phrases like 'natural-born city', 'landscape of capital', and 'watershed of competition'. They reinforce Cronon's investigation of the city as *second nature*: an assemblage of mingled natural and human endeavour, from dredged rivers to siloed grain, animated by (and intended to serve) the circulation of commodities and capital. The metropolitan empire that Cronon traces, composed of cities and their networked hinterlands, operates most basically through 'the extension of market relations into the ways that human beings used land' (Cronon, 1991, p.53). Yet even Cronon's study, with its attention to physical landscape, only briefly considers the abstraction of land into property – a process that receives most attention in recounting the story of early settlers and the purchase of land from Native Americans – before passing swiftly to more studied concentration on the abstraction of other natural products, such as grain. The rivers of transmogrifying wheat that flow in and out of Chicago seem to pass over solid ground, the material terrain securely fixed in place for the purposes of capital accumulation. Indeed, in much urban environmental history, land remains something of a bit actor supporting the primary players of the city's 'metabolism': water, waste, rivers, energy, parks, and animal infrastructures (Gandy, 2004; Massard-Guilbaud and Thorsheim, 2007; Muller and Tarr, 2019; Taylor and Trentmann, 2011).

Significant recent research on urban land is more attentive to the flux and undecideability that attends the process of attempting to fix its parameters with property. Land is a central category – an actor, a product, and mode of governance – in Debjani Bhattacharyya's study of the formation and development of Calcutta, the British administrative capital in nineteenth-century India. In her study of the history (and future) of its development as a deltaic city, Bhattacharyya 'conceives of the built environment of Calcutta as sedimentation of historical time, silt and human design' (Bhattacharyya, 2018, p.3). Her study centres the ecology of the city, the 'soaked' landscape of fluid exchanges of water and land, in the history of the city's evolution, which advances through legal boundary-making, physical landscape interventions, and the consequent establishment of landed property as a speculative commodity. The slowness of riverine changes in the locale that the British set out to make their capital encourages a consideration of the deeper time of real estate, while the constant flux of the wetland setting highlights both the particular task of property as a technology of fixity and the agency of an environment that can escape and overpower its confines.

Bhattacharyya's study alerts us to important considerations in the history of urban real estate and imperial cities. The first is that the legal processes by which various elements of the natural landscape – land, rivers, and the soaked spaces between – become property must be approached not only through an assessment of law and colonial governance, but also by appreciating how markets and economics intervene in these juridical processes – indeed, how they are deployed as elements of a 'market governance' that complements imperial juridical and police power. In the urban setting in particular, property must be appreciated as a legal *and* economic artefact. The process of making colonial Calcutta, she argues, involves the construction of property *primarily* in terms of its economic imaginary. This is a second important consideration: that the creation of real estate markets is a transformation in ways of seeing urban land that profoundly reshapes the conditions of possibility for a city's development. The process of 'propertizing' in the colonial urban context was also a process of forgetting, of suppressing 'hydrological memory' and thus changing the forces viewed as central in the organization of urban space and urban dwellers (Bhattacharyya, 2018, p.171). The commoditization of urban property meant changing swamps into housing-in-waiting – a radical transformation in mental dispositions that serve as precondition for new patterns of land use and governance.

Because it is a technology of both governance and capital accumulation, real estate enters the archive through bureaucratic practices of regularization and control. It is a scheme of colonial authority. Yet Bhattacharyya offers an example of how to think with real estate outside – or, in addition to – such disciplinary spaces. By attending to the physical realities of Calcutta's fluid topography, as well as to the multiplicity of mental and cultural worlds of property that that topography hosts, real estate can be more readily understood as a technique of constantly attenuated, constantly becoming, fixity. As she writes, 'keeping alive this temporariness and flux within the landscape challenges the permanence that bolsters our thinking around law, land market, and design' (Bhattacharyya, 2018, p.31). It restores real estate to the dynamism of its life off the colonial ledger; the flip from swamp to dry land, from unreal to real estate, figures as one moment in a contested process of commoditization.

The argument that a vital part of the function and experience of urban real estate lies in its simultaneous incompleteness and definitiveness is fruitful even for seemingly solid terrain, such as the apartment complexes studied by historian Nikhil Rao (2013) in his account of Bombay's suburbanization in the twentieth century. Like Bhattacharyya, Rao begins with the operations of imperial administrators as they set about renovating the urban landscape, starting with the emergence of the Bombay Improvement Trust as a suburban land developer in the early twentieth century. His account centres the construction of urban property and its markets. The Trust, he shows, was guided in its land acquisition and development policies by the desire to establish a smoothly functioning land market that would facilitate its renovation schemes. In the process, it effects a transformation in the perception of land at the urban edge, changing it from agricultural territory to land 'awaiting development', and so properly subject to urbanizing interventions (Rao, 2013, p.23). (We are reminded of the temporal effect of real-estate-as-property: under its sway, the urban is something that extends in time, as well as space.) The residential buildings that soon came to populate the lots the Trust cleared and sold to developers were shaped less by design than by localized circumstances in the property market – namely, its cycles of boom and bust in the 1920s. But in addition to careful reconstruction of how the Trust worked through a real estate market that was partially of its own creation, Rao adds an appreciation of real estate as a lived space – not only a mapped or dreamed or administered one – that helps account for its agency in the morphological as well as social and cultural processes of suburbanization. The production and material form of the 'Bombay flat' becomes the basis for a distinctly Indian, lower-middle-class, urban identity, tied to particular spaces, living habits, and caste networks.

Approaching these flats and urban districts from the vantage of real estate clarifies vectors by which land was commoditized in a particular context and identifies previously understudied forces central to the formation of urban and community identity. What it means to be a city dweller and political subject in modern Bombay can be illuminated through real estate's multi-scalar existence: an artefact at once of state enforcement, of private sector mobilization, and of material structure. But what happens when that existence is less stable, or less conventional, than might be outwardly apparent? In fact, Rao's approach leads him to a fascinating, generative case of uncertain 'propertizing' that significantly complicates these scales of relations. The connection of these low-rise buildings with middle-class identity, he argues, was achieved through their architectural form (importantly, their self-contained, private washroom facilities); through their turn to ownership over rental tenure as the century progressed; and, most importantly, through the fact that their construction was typically shepherded by caste-exclusionary cooperative housing societies, cementing links between the material form of urban living and specific community identities. Yet remarkably, the merchandise upon which this identity (partially) relied was doubly opaque (Rao, 2012). In the first instance, the 'ownership flat' – an apartment that is owned rather than rented – was legally undefined; it only partially fulfilled the technical conditions of real estate, which it nevertheless was popularly assumed to constitute. Second, the ownership of land upon which these buildings were erected also frequently did not align with the understanding of flat owners – when they were concerned with it, which they often were not.

This finding leads to suggestive questions, both about the nature of urban development and about the kind of political identity that this 'real' estate might inform. If there is an 'outside' to the process of urban becoming, in this instance, it may be located in the heart of the city itself, underneath its defining architectural form and layered in the neglected paperwork of registry files. What does this instability signify for a political culture and possessive politics that retains important links between ownership, citizenship, and bourgeois belonging (Appadurai, 2001; Harvey, 2008)? Such questions have been particularly important in the Indian context, in which the role of the (propertied) middle class in performing the boundaries of political capacity is subject to ongoing examination (Anjaria, 2009; Hazareesingh, 2000). But they also signal key avenues of study and comparison for other urban settings. The propertied view of the city is a view from *somewhere*; in revealing the disjuncture between enjoyment of property and legally enforceable property rights, Rao's research gives the lie to the global fashion for (putatively liberating) property titling schemes, showing that title is perhaps neither a necessary nor sufficient condition to guarantee occupancy and use of urban land. A similar dynamic can be seen in rental markets, as in those of contemporary Cairo, where 44 per cent of households rent. Split between a segment of older rent-controlled tenancies (39 per cent of total housing) and newer leases freed from regulation (10 per cent), the majority of urban residents express high feelings of security in their tenure – despite significant pressure on owners to reclaim the property values previously suppressed by the state (Sims, 2010). In both cases, whose possession is pathologized and whose protected is class politics: a deeply political gesture of inclusion and exclusion.

Nowhere are these dynamics more evident than in the locus of urbanization that typically preoccupies studies of land use in the Global South: informal settlements, often glossed as slums, which stand in for the region's frequently pathologized megacities (Roy, 2011). Brazil's *favelas* exemplify the role of real-estate-as-property in shaping urban form and politics. These zones of (seemingly) haphazard settlement, populated by the poor (often racially marginalized) classes of the country's large cities, are characterized by uncertain property claims, substandard construction, and limited provision of public goods and services, which perpetuate the economic and political disenfranchisement of their residents. They date to the late-nineteenth century and have grown throughout the twentieth, sometimes at faster rates than the formal city, of which they form an integral part (Perlman, 2004). Their origin, as historian Brodwyn Fischer (2008) demonstrates, lies in customary practices of land occupation and appropriation in Brazil. A complicated layering of legal claims to property originating in the Portuguese imperial period generated situations of genuine uncertainty with regards to land ownership, setting up conflicting bases upon which legitimate property claims might proceed. Public land might become private property on the basis of productive occupation, periods of effective possession, or – from the early Brazilian imperial period – on the basis of purchase. Boundaries were vague, custom and consensus weighed significantly but unevenly. That settlement – by rich and poor alike – thus frequently transpired on 'uncertain ground' was predictable; when it was remarked upon at all, most considered it an ordinary mode of fabricating the city.[12] From the 1920s, however, its contradictions were weaponized as opportunistic landowners and entrepreneurs pushed formal property claims as a means of dispossessing residents of increasingly valuable urban land.

What assembled these pervasive uncertainties into distinct and identifiable zones of informal settlement populated overwhelmingly by the poor was the fact that such patterns presented valuable opportunities for manipulation, negotiation, and profit for a host of interests, from residents and landowners to speculators and politicians. Far from growing up in the interstices of official settlement, many of Rio's favelas began as (informal) real estate investments on the part of prominent families; Fischer speculates that the logic of profiteering animating favelas may have grown from business practices pioneered in the tenement business of the city centre (Fischer, 2008, p.395 n.101). Rather than a non- or sub-market space, the informal settlement is constitutively linked to real estate markets and real estate capital. A recent study of the emergence of an early favela in the planned city of Belo Horizonte reveals how it was directly created to further the state's interest in creating a marketized property for real estate in the new provincial capital; planners allocated workers and their housing forms – officially barred from that market – to an adjacent informal settlement area (McDonald, 2019). In both contexts, planned and unplanned, incidental extralegal settlement became indispensable to urban development and politics. Residents secured cheap shelter, and the very uncertainty of their claims – which made them both vulnerable and valuable to profiteering middlemen – made them useful as a group of potential voters whose loyalty could be

---

[12] Informal settlements emerge as a named, notable, and problematized phenomenon at a distinct historical conjuncture in the early twentieth century (Fischer, 2014).

secured on the cheap. This symbiosis (such as it was) did not proceed peacefully; violence and brutality were central to its operation, and inequality its *sine qua non*. But a complex web of dependence has secured its durability as a mode of urbanization and urbanity.

In the place of the informal settlement as an inevitable, ahistorical by-product of unwieldy urbanization and modernization, then, emerges informality as political and economic device, honed to local circumstance and serving the ends – political, economic, experiential – of specific constituencies. Too often, the fine-grained research necessary to achieve this understanding has not been the rule. Writing in response to increasingly fashionable 'slum studies' literature, Fischer laments the thinness of our historical appreciation of these communities: 'For most places, at most times, we still do not know how poor informal cities came into being, what range of ties bound them to their urban contexts, what allowed them to persist over successive generations, or what their presence has done to transform Latin American or Brazilian urbanity' (Fischer, 2014, p.11). Fischer is suggesting a much richer, more polyvalent framework for studying the function and meaning of informal settlements. It indicates the need to understand cities from the informal settlement *outward* – to problematize the 'formal' as much as the 'informal', to fit them into a common analytic frame, attributing both the status of historical subject, endowed with historical contingency.

Such study would accomplish at least two critical tasks. First, it would help urban historians to think *with* but also *beyond* the practices of dispossession that are at work in the property-making and -claiming of formal/informal border zones. It encourages a history of presence – of occupation, resistance, and endurance. The potentialities and practices of expulsion inherent in real-estate-as-property are too vicious and omnipresent to be laid aside, but they exist in dialectic with real estate's capacity for material, legal, and social embedding. Second, it offers a methodology for replying to the call of one of the foremost scholarly authorities on informality, Ananya Roy, when she argues that approaching informality as a mode of urban governance – as a political process as well as a spatial formation – requires appreciating the production of historical difference (Roy, 2016). Cities perform much of the work of state making; they administer access to services, to benefits and entitlements of citizenship and subjecthood, and they craft and enforce regulation across multiple scales. Property is a key mode by which they govern. How uneven zones of rights, access, dwelling, and value are inscribed through and across land is the core of modern urbanization, and a process that requires empirical investigation. Addressing a settlement's historical rootedness increases the likelihood that processes of differentiation come to the fore.

As suggested by the opening framing of this section, the processes reviewed here are of consequence to more than urban history. The commoditization of nature and land via property is intrinsic to empire and capital accumulation, and of particular weight in the ongoing conjoined crisis of climate and capitalism (Moore, 2015). Cities can be placed at the centre of these processes, historical and contemporary, as both targets and amplifiers. As Dossal writes, evoking the broad implications of urban property transformations: 'private property and the emergence of a capitalist land market in Bombay rank among the most significant developments in the mid-nineteenth century' (Dossal, 2010, p.105). Property, like capital, should be understood not as a thing, but as a set of relations, and as a *process* of establishing and (re)assembling those relations. These relations are shaped by – and often useful to – inequalities of power, which is what makes property such a fundamental tool for opening the political economies of cities. From this vantage, the city – not only its people, not only its buildings, but its very ground – is revealed as a mobile landscape. In attempting to fix what is mobile – as well as to mobilize what is (apparently) fixed – real-estate-as-property generates material and immaterial terrains for capital accumulation and governance. It also fabricates a landscape of multiple temporalities. The process of propertizing is a process that changes land into development- or housing-in-waiting; it institutes a future orientation to a terrain and mode of occupation, an expectation, while also imposing a pause, a waiting, into which great uncertainty (but also opportunity for profit) can build. (Again: consider the snapshot of the waqf and its relations at the introduction of this section.) With this, we arrive at a series of reflections that somewhat escapes the task set for this subsection by its title and juxtaposition with the previous discussion. By attending to the histories, in distinct urban settings, of the making of real-estate-as-property, the fluidity of the propertied form and the limits to its fixity are keenly evident.

This section has focused on cities in the Global South by virtue of the strength and creativity of recent scholarship focusing on land use. Yet this may leave the impression that the qualities of real-estate-as-property that make it both so influential in urban development and fruitful as an analytic lens for scholarly work are restricted to these urban contexts. This is not at all the case, though scholarship on processes of propertizing in cities of the Global North is thinner, and the framework of informality is rarely stretched to incorporate analyses that cross the putative North-South divide (Harris, 2018; Jindrich, 2017). Nevertheless, squatting and 'homesteading' have been important twentieth-century urban phenomena in Europe and the United States as well (Goldstein, 2017; Kwak, 2021; Vasudevan, 2017; Ward, 2002) (Figure 15). Consider the example of Paris, the icon of urban modernity, whose avenues and apartment

Figure 15 From company housing to squats to cooperative: these houses on
Bonnington Square, London, were originally constructed in the 1870s as
accommodation for railway workers. The area was bought up by the Greater
London Council after the Second World War, and empty houses were occupied
by squatters in the 1980s. The square escaped demolition when the residents
came together to create a housing cooperative.

Image © London Metropolitan Archives (City of London)

buildings epitomize an unproblematic ordering of commoditized and marketized space. Even here, multiple and overlapping property claims and contested
reformulations of real-estate-as-property are, upon inspection, evident and
influential. For example, the sales contracts of nationalized Church and
emigré property, appropriated and sold through the Revolution down to 1815,
contained clauses referencing future urban development plans that obliged
acquirers to sacrifice their property to public purposes if their lots intersected
with approved development schemes. These *clauses domaniales* created a kind
of public lien against a property, a spectre of revolutionary acquisition that hung
over subsequent purchasers. Expropriation for public purpose was itself
a conventional practice, strengthened throughout the century – famously
extended to facilitate the massive urban reforms of Haussmannization in the
1850s. Recalling Nikhil Rao's study of the 'ownership flat' in twentieth-century
Bombay, in the 1920s and 30s in France, the construction of new condominium

apartments occurred without firm legal grounding, requiring legislation to regularize possession of a 'cube of air' well after developments had spread and sales had taken off (Yates, 2011). The resulting *co-propriétés* or co-owned buildings of owner-occupied apartments support an entire industry of professional managers and legal specialists to sort ownership conflicts. Finally, the registration of real property sales, a *desiderata* of modern property regimes according to generations of reformers, was not required in France until 1955. Indeed, reviewing proposals to make registration mandatory at the end of the nineteenth century, French property observers sniffed that such measures might be 'necessary for new countries', but would thoroughly disturb the venerable traditions of 'a perfectly civilized country' like France (Ministère du Commerce, 1889, p.11).

The general definition of informality invoked by Richard Harris – 'those actions of economic agents that fail to adhere to the established institutional rules or are denied their protection' – certainly serves to expand the concept's purchase beyond the slum as metonym of informality (Harris, 2018, p.267). For example, while the proliferation of paperwork it entailed would not conform to the experience of 'informality' as it has been discussed above, the predatory and discriminatory marketing of mortgages in the lead-up to the 2008 financial crisis, which led to the most significant foreclosure event in the history of the United States, certainly created and relied on the uncertainties of tenure that constitutively animate real estate 'ownership', with its intrinsic dialectics of fixity and dispossession (Stout, 2019; White et al., 2014). The aggressive extension of credit to 'sub-prime' clients suggests failures of adherence to and protection of institutional rules, especially where that category intersects with racialized populations (Wyly et al., 2006). For all its significance, the size of this foreclosure episode pales in comparison to the intergenerational damage inflicted upon African-American wealth through the discriminatory urban process in the United States known as 'redlining', after the mapping practices by which federal agencies and their private partners purposively denied equal access to housing finance to spatially-designated Black communities. Also a 'Herculean' effort of paperwork, redlining transformed Black urban property into a less fungible (and so less valuable) asset by limiting its liquidity and transferability, creating a hierarchy of tenures (Connolly et al., 2018, p.510). This unevenness enhanced opportunities for profit for white proprietors and the white real estate industry. Practices like sales on contracts – essentially installment payment plans for houses made available to Black purchasers who could not otherwise obtain mortgage financing – created lucrative vulnerabilities; 'owners' who missed one payment could be evicted from a house, which could then be remarketed to another family (Satter, 2009).

In both cases – one of structural credit denial, the other of aggressive provisioning – these predatory propertizing practices frequently conformed to the letter of the law; this is clearly an important difference from the ambiguous legal regimes that define many informal settlements. And there are other vital differences: in formats of land commoditization (between, say, slum regularization in Mumbai and the development of sub-prime fuelled suburbs in New Mexico); in the modes by which state (and non-state) violence is enacted and its extent; in the force of displacement and its consequences for communities and citizenship. Without replicating unhelpful analogies between the 'slum' and the 'ghetto' perpetuated by the global developmental 'cultures of poverty' discourse in the 1960s (Fischer, 2014), there is scope for bringing selective consideration of state-sanctioned (and profit-oriented) policies of spatialized and racialized (dis)possession within a common frame (Roy, 2017). An urban history attentive to the dynamics of real estate would enable a more globalized perspective on urban processes without presuming or requiring congruent urban outcomes.

The case studies of modes of viewing urban history through the lens of real estate tested here – markets and landed property – are only a fraction of possible entry points. 'Real estate as buildings' could tell urban history from the vantage of a typical urban form, such as the bungalow, the apartment building, or the housing tower; analysis could plunge inside built forms, opening domestic spaces, interrogating architectural and design history and attending particularly to the gendered qualities of real estate production and use (Hernandez, 2010 11; King, 2005; Kuchta, 2010; Lasner, 2012; Rudolph, 2015.) Acknowledging the significance of different economic regimes, this analysis could distinguish between the divergent circumstances and meanings of outwardly similar urban forms, such as the gated community. Or, scanning outward, it could adopt the perspective of mega-projects such as the Prudential Tower in Boston or Chungking Mansions in Hong Kong, crafting spatial biographies of significant development ventures (Matthews, 2011; Rubin, 2012). 'Real estate as capital' could open local and transnational histories of financing the built environment of a city, provide opportunities for accounts of the lived experience of speculative real estate, and incorporate analyses of how these circuits of investment and profit have created new urban subjects as well as new vectors of exclusion and political contestation (Aalbers, 2012; Goldman, 2011; Pellandini-Simányi et al., 2015). 'Real estate as relation' could tackle themes from the dynamics of landlord-tenant relations to the financialization of rental housing to the affective register of homeownership, inserting the personal and embodied experiences of real property into the spectrum of cultural facets of the urban experience (Fields, 2017). All of these approaches would borrow from their cognate urban specialties: architectural history; urban planning; critical urban geography; social and cultural history. But by insisting on the relations of proprietorship, capital, displacement, and possession contained in real estate, the result is a historically-informed political economy of cities and the urban, one whose embeddedness in the processes scaling the local and the global is specified, actor-centred, and oriented toward comparison.

5 Conclusion

At first glance, urban real estate defies a transnational or global history. It is materially and legally *unmovable*: fixed in specific locations and constituted by the laws of particular nation-states. Planners and money and people might circulate, but real estate stays in place. As agricultural land, it produces slowly; as buildings, it locks away pensions and inheritances and savings: 'Safe as houses'. Popular discussions of real estate in advanced capitalist countries are mimetic and repetitive (across time and borders), returning consistently to its aura of perennial value regardless of recurrent booms, busts, and displacements. This fixity has long been its key virtue in the eyes of owners, users, governments, and capital that can profit from such rootedness. However, this intractability tells only part of real estate's story. The other part is *mobilization*: engine and conduit for the circulation of capital, a mode of appropriation and dispossession creating a churn of inhabitants, owners, and users. Real estate as this volume defines it is both product and agent of political, economic, and cultural globalization.

This Element began with the suggestion that real estate has been largely without a history, and has sought to provide perspectives and inspiration necessary to address this absence. Injunctions for urban historians to 'follow the money' are not new, nor have they been entirely ignored. From Sam Bass Warner Jr's urging historians to spend more time with 'ownership and speculation' (1978, p.vii) to Lynn Hollen Lees's concern about 'the comparative lack of attention to social and economic processes' (2015, p.593) in contemporary urban scholarship, there is a shared endorsement of particular methodologies and goals for urban history. These are calls for anchoring urban history in the 'real' and the tangible, even as – as Lees acknowledges – awareness of the transnational and global scale of the urban has grown. They cleave to the paperwork and genealogies that result from property's status as an essential concern of western legal traditions and state archives. 'Armed with the name of the owner', Warner writes, he assaults 'that organized morass, the Registry of Deeds', emerging somewhat cowed by 'a giant index of hundreds of volumes for the years 1630-1899 [that] guides one from the man granting away the title to his property to the man who received it', so voluminous that ultimately it 'can only be sampled' (Warner, 1978, p.190).

Real estate histories certainly demand this intensive and enterprising archival work – it is one of the signal virtues of the approach, especially when understood as part of the work of restoring historical agency to sites and groups to which it has been denied. It is also how the specificities of real estate relations are tracked, their importance tested, and a flattening of its operations and impact avoided. (If we want to know *how* a real estate speculator in 1860s Tokyo can be usefully compared to one in 1890s Rio de Janeiro or 1950s Baltimore – or whether, to take exemplars central to David Harvey's work, Paris's Baron Haussmann and New York's Robert Moses are interchangeable figures – this empirical foundation is essential.) But a broader conceptualization of real estate, constructed from the theoretical perspectives and comparative contexts introduced in this volume, is important to combat the gravitational pull of those archives towards the local and the 'merely' empirical. Approaching real estate not only as a thing, or even only as capital, but also as a technique of governance that organizes spaces and populations allows it to inform urban histories that *problematize* appropriate scales of analysis and *extend beyond* the economic or the material. Real estate's key modalities are differentiation and (dis)possession; its history intersects with and undergirds violent operations of power that constitute racial, class, and gender inequalities. From this vantage, Warner's ledger toggles between historical source and historical technology: erasing or marginalizing some actors, narratives, and episodes, even while constituting others. Denaturalizing real estate as an economic artefact, freeing it from the simplifying spell of commoditization, allows its social and political complexity to generate new questions and answers about the multi-scalar relationships constituting everyday urban environments.

That the history of real estate relations has not played a significant role in revising existing narratives as the field of urban history has become increasingly global is unfortunate. The circumstances of the 2008 global financial crisis and recession have somewhat checked this oversight, generating vital empirical and theoretical research on the centrality of real estate to the financialization of the global economy. Yet the nature of this scholarly focus risks real estate being stuck in the present tense: over-informed by present-day concerns, and unhelpfully bound up with shallow histories of neoliberalism. Much of this critical literature traffics in the assumption that financialization and its mobilization of real estate capital are uniquely post-1970s phenomena, and so miscasts the nature and politics of these processes. A renewed, historicized, and globalized engagement with real estate in the modern city has perhaps never seemed so urgent.

Real estate's urban histories also offer arguments for global historians to take cities as more central objects of analysis. Too many global historians need to be reminded of the locatedness of global processes – of the notion, as Michael Geyer and Charles Bright articulated in a now classic article, that 'the condition of globality has always been organized locally, in one place after the other, according to particular circumstances and conditions that happen to obtain' (1995, p.1057). The degree to which the urban has figured as a specific scale and condition for global history remains uneven – stymied, perhaps, by the thickness of the specificities of contexts that congeal around cities as particular places or cases. If we are to learn more about how the connections between spatializations of distinct processes were acted out historically, how they were enmeshed and separated and engaged differing agencies, an approach that accounts for cities as places where people and institutions managed these processes is necessary (Middell and Naumann, 2010). And real estate as this volume has approached it powerfully exemplifies these movements and manifestations of scale. Its constitution reflects the collision of impulses to de-territorialize and re-territorialize that define the contemporary (and historical) process of world-making – the management, as Geyer and Bright put it, of worldwide processes of mobilization and unsettlement (of people, things, ideas) via efforts to selectively settle or control those movements. But what's more, it can keep the global historian tethered to the realm of experience, from which the discipline's most profound contributions stem. In this way, the intimate modes and personal stakes of belonging and possession that are activated by real estate's relations can maintain a critical foothold in stories of market abstraction and circulation.

References

Aalbers, M., ed. (2012). *Subprime Cities: The Political Economy of Mortgage Markets*, Chichester, UK: Wiley-Blackwell.

(2008). The Financialization of Home and the Mortgage Market Crisis. *Competition & Change*, 12(2), 148–166.

Abbenhuis, M. and Morrell, G. W. (2020). *The First Age of Industrial Globalization: An International History 1815–1918*, London: Bloomsbury.

Abbott, C. (1981). *Boosters and Businessmen: Popular Economic Thought and Urban Growth in the Antebellum Middle West*, Westport, CT: Greenwood Press.

Abu-Lughod, J. (1980). *Rabat: Urban Apartheid in Morocco*, Princeton: Princeton University Press.

Angelo, H. (2017). From the City Lens toward Urbanisation as a Way of Seeing: Country/City Binaries on an Urbanizing Planet. *Urban Studies*, 54(1), 158–178.

Anjaria, J. S. (2009). Guardians of the Bourgeois City: Citizenship, Public Space, and Middle-Class Activism in Mumbai. *City & Community*, 8(4), 391–406.

Appadurai, A. (2001). Deep Democracy: Urban Governmentality and the Horizon of Politics. *Environment and Urbanization*, 13(2), 23–43.

Argersinger, J. A. E. (2010). Contested Visions of American Democracy: Citizenship, Public Housing, and the International Arena. *Journal of Urban History*, 36(6), 792–813.

Arrighi, G. (2010 [1994]). *The Long Twentieth Century: Money, Power, and the Origins of our Times*, London: Verso.

Baer, J. A. (1993). Tenant Mobilization and the 1907 Rent Strike in Buenos Aires. *The Americas*, 49(3), 343–368.

Bailleux de Marisy, A. (1881). Les Nouvelles sociétés foncières. Mœurs Financières de la France IV. *Revue des deux mondes* (November 15), 432–452.

Balakrishnan, S. (2019). Placing and Spacing the Dead in Colonial Accra. *The Metropole: Official Blog of the Urban History Association*. Accessed 13 February 2020. https://themetropole.blog/2019/11/25/placing-and-spacing-the-dead-in-colonial-accra/.

Ballantyne, T. and Burton, A. (2012). *Empires and the Reach of the Global, 1870–1945*, Cambridge, MA: Harvard University Press.

Banner, S. (2011). *American Property: A History of How, Why, and What We Own*, Cambridge, MA: Harvard University Press.

(2007). *How the Indians Lost Their Land: Law and Power on the Frontier*, Cambridge, MA: Harvard University Press.

Beauregard, R. (2007). More Than Sector Theory: Homer Hoyt's Contributions to Planning Knowledge. *Journal of Planning History*, 6(3), 248–271.

Beckert, S. (2016). The New History of Capitalism. In J. Kocka and M. van der Linden, eds., *Capitalism: The Reemergence of a Historical Concept*, London: Bloomsbury, 235–250.

Béguin, K. and Lyon-Caen, N. (2018). Dans la chaleur des enchères: Adjudications et prix des immeubles à Paris aux XVIIe et XVIIIe siècles. *Revue d'histoire moderne et contemporaine*, 65(1), 144–166.

Beverley, E. (2018). Territoriality in Motion: Waqf and Hyderabad State. *The Muslim World*, 109(1), 630–651.

Bhandar, B. (2018). *Colonial Lives of Property: Law, Land, and Racial Regimes of Ownership*, Durham: Duke University Press.

Bhattacharyya, D. (2018). *Empire and Ecology in the Bengal Delta: The Making of Calcutta*, Cambridge: Cambridge University Press.

Bigon, L. (2016). Bubonic Plague, Colonial Ideologies, and Urban Planning Policies: Dakar, Lagos, and Kumasi. *Planning Perspectives*, 31(2), 205–226.

Bissell, W. (2011). *Urban Design, Chaos, and Colonial Power in Zanzibar*, Bloomington: Indiana University Press.

Blackmar, E. (2013). Inheriting Property and Debt: From Family Security to Corporate Accumulation. In M. Zakim and G. J. Kornblith, eds., *Capitalism Takes Command: The Social Transformation of Nineteenth-Century America*, Chicago: University of Chicago Press, 93–117.

(2005). Of REITs and Rights: Absentee Ownership in the Periphery. In J. M. Diefendorf and K. Dorsey, eds., *City, Country, Empire: Landscapes in Environmental History*, Pittsburgh: University of Pittsburgh Press, 81–98.

(1985). *Manhattan for Rent, 1785–1850*, Ithaca, NY: Cornell University Press.

Blatman-Thomas, N. and Porter, L. (2019). Placing Property: Theorizing the Urban from Settler Colonial Cities. *International Journal of Urban and Regional Research*, 43(1), 30–45.

Blaufarb, R. (2016). *The Great Demarcation: The French Revolution and the Invention of Modern Property*, New York: Oxford University Press.

Blomley, N. (2014). *Unsettling the City: Urban Land and the Politics of Property*, London: Routledge.

Bonneval, L. and Robert, F. (2019). *De la rente immobilière à la finance: la Société de la rue Impériale (Lyon 1854–2004)*, Paris: ENS Éditions.

Bourdieu, P. (2005). *Social Structures of the Economy*, trans. C. Turner, Cambridge: Polity.

Brady, M. (2018). The Forgotten History of Metes and Bounds. *Yale Law Journal*, 128, 872–953.

Brenner, N., ed. (2014). *Implosions/Explosions: Towards a Study of Planetary Urbanization*, Berlin: Jovis.

Buck-Morss, S. (1989). *The Dialectics of Seeing: Walter Benjamin and the Arcades Project*, Cambridge, MA: MIT Press.

Burley, D. G. (1988). The Keepers of the Gate: The Inequality of Property Ownership during the Winnipeg Real Estate Boom of 1881–1882. *Urban History Review/Revue d'histoire urbaine*, 17(2), 63–76.

Buzzelli, M. and Harris, R. (2006). Cities as the Industrial Districts of Housebuilding. *International Journal of Urban and Regional Research*, 30(4), 894–917.

Casson, C. and Casson, M. (2016). Location, Location, Location? Analysing Property Rents in Medieval Gloucester. *The Economic History Review*, 69 (2), 575–599.

Cavalcanti, M. (2014). Threshold Markets: The Production of Real Estate Value between the Favela and the Pavement. In B. Fischer, B. McCann and J. Auyero, eds., *Cities from Scratch: Poverty and Informality in Urban Latin America*, Durham, NC: Duke University Press, 208–237.

Çelik, Z. (1997). *Urban Forms and Colonial Confrontations: Algiers Under French Rule*, Berkeley: University of California Press.

Chakrabarty, D. (2000). *Provincializing Europe: Postcolonial Thought and Historical Difference*, Princeton: Princeton University Press.

Chauvard, J-F. (2005). *La Circulation des biens à Venise: Stratégies patrimoniales et marché immobilier, 1600–1750*, Rome: Ecole française de Rome.

Chehabi, H. E. (2019). The Rise of the Middle Class in Iran before the Second World War. In C. Dejung, D. Motadel and J. Osterhammel, eds., *The Global Bourgeoisie: The Rise of the Middle Classes in the Age of Empire*, Princeton: Princeton University Press, 43–63.

Chelcea, L. (2012). The Housing Question and the State-Socialist Answer: City, Class, and State Remaking in 1950s Bucharest. *International Journal of Urban and Regional Research*, 36(2), 281–296.

Chhabria, S. (2019). *Making the Modern Slum: The Power of Capital in Colonial Bombay*, Seattle, WA : University of Washington Press.

Choko, M. (1997). Investment or Family Home? Housing Ownership in Paris at the Turn of the Twentieth Century. *Journal of Urban History*, 23(5), 531–568.

Choko, M. and Harris, R. (1990). The Local Culture of Property: A Comparative History of Housing Tenure in Montreal and Toronto. *Annals of the Association of American Geographers*, 80(1), 73–95.

Christopher, A. J. (1985). Patterns of British Overseas Investment in Land, 1885–1913. *Transactions of the Institute of British Geographers*, 10(4), 452–466.

Chu, C. (2013). Combating Nuisance: Sanitation, Regulation, and the Politics of Property in Colonial Hong Kong. In R. Peckham and D. Pomfret, eds., *Imperial Contagions: Medicine, Hygiene, and Cultures of Planning in Asia*, Hong Kong: Hong Kong University Press, 17–36.

Chuan, H. (1979). The Economic Crisis of 1883 as Seen in the Failure of Hsü Jun's Real Estate Business in Shanghai. In C. Hou and T. Yu, eds., *Modern Chinese Economic History: Proceedings of the Conference on Modern Chinese Economic History, Academia Sinica, Taipei, Taiwan, Republic of China, August 26–29, 1977*, Taipei: The Institute of Economics, 493–498.

Connolly, N. D. B. (2014). *A World More Concrete: Real Estate and the Remaking of Jim Crow South Florida*, Chicago: University of Chicago Press.

Connolly, N. D. B., Winling, L., Nelson, R. K. and Marciano, R. (2018). Mapping Inequality: 'Big Data' Meets Social History in the Story of Redlining. In I. Gregory, D. DeBats and D. Lafreniere, eds., *The Routledge Companion to Spatial History*, London: Routledge, 502–524.

Cronon, W. (1991). *Nature's Metropolis: Chicago and the Great West*, New York: W. W. Norton and Company.

Crossick, G. (2000). Meanings of Property and the World of the Petite Bourgeoisie. In J. Stobart and A. Owens, eds., *Urban Fortunes: Property and Inheritance in the Town, 1700–1900*, Aldershot, UK: Ashgate, 50–78.

Cupers, K. (2014). *The Social Project: Housing Postwar France*, Minneapolis: University of Minnesota Press.

Daumard, A. (1965). *Maisons de Paris et propriétaires parisiens au XIXe siècle (1809–1880)*, Paris: Editions Cujas.

Daunton, M. (1983). *House and Home in the Victorian City: Working Class Housing, 1850–1914*, London: Edward Arnold.

Davis, D. E. (2005). Cities in Global Context: A Brief Intellectual History. *International Journal of Urban and Regional Research*, 29(1), 92–109.

Dejung, C, Motadel, D. and Osterhammel, J. (2019). *The Global Bourgeoisie: The Rise of the Middle Classes in the Age of Empire*, Princeton: Princeton University Press.

Demissie, F., ed. (2009). *Colonial Architecture and Urbanism in Africa*, Burlington, VT: Ashgate.

Desmond, M. (2016). *Evicted: Poverty and Profit in the American City*, New York City: Broadway Books.

Di Martino, P. (2012). Rome Wasn't Built in a Day: Lobbies, Institutions, and Speculation in the 1880s Building Fever. *Urban History*, 39(3), 471–489.

Documents relatifs au régime hypothécaire et aux réformes qui ont été proposées (1844). 3 vols., Paris: Imprimerie Royale.

Dorries, H., Hugill, D. and Tomiak, J. (2019). Racial Capitalism and the Production of Settler Colonial Cities. *Geoforum*. Accessed 3 February 2020. https://doi.org/10.1016/j.geoforum.2019.07.016.

Doshi, S. (2013). The Politics of the Evicted: Redevelopment, Subjectivity, and Difference in Mumbai's Slum Frontier. *Antipode*, 45(4), 844–865.

Dossal, M. (2010). *Theatre of Conflict, City of Hope: Mumbai, 1660 to Present Times*, New Delhi: Oxford University Press.

Doucet, M. and Weaver, J. (1984). The North American Shelter Business, 1860–1920. *The Business History Review*, 58(2), 234–262.

(1991). *Housing the North American City*, Montreal: McGill-Queens University Press.

Dyos, H. J. (1982). The Speculative Builders and Developers of Victorian London. In D. Cannadine and D. Reeder, eds., *Exploring the Urban Past: Essays in Urban History by H. J. Dyos*, Cambridge: Cambridge University Press, 154–178.

Echenberg, M. (2010). *Plague Ports: The Global Urban Impact of Bubonic Plague, 1894–1901*, New York: New York University Press.

Eichholtz, P. (1997). A Long-Run House Price Index: The Herengracht Index, 1628–1973. *Real Estate Economics*, 25(2), 175–192.

El-Kazaz, S. (2018). Building 'Community' and Markets in Contemporary Cairo. *Comparative Studies in Society and History*, 60(2), 476–505.

Englander, D. (1983). *Landlord and Tenant in Urban Britain, 1838–1918*, Oxford: Oxford University Press.

Everett, P. (2019). *Urban Transformations: From Liberalism to Corporatism in Greater Berlin, 1871–1933*, Toronto: University of Toronto Press.

Ewen, S. and Saunier, P-Y., eds. (2008). *Another Global City: Historical Explorations into the Transnational Municipal Moment, 1850–2000*, Basingstoke: Palgrave.

Fields, D. (2017). Unwilling Subjects of Financialization. *International Journal of Urban and Regional Research*, 41(4), 588–603.

Fischer, B. (2008). *A Poverty of Rights: Citizenship and Inequality in Twentieth-Century Rio de Janeiro*, Stanford: Stanford University Press.

    (2014). A Century in the Present Tense: Crisis, Politics, and the Intellectual History of Brazil's Informal Cities. In B. Fischer, B. McCann and J. Auyero, eds., *Cities from Scratch: Poverty and Informality in Urban Latin America*, Durham, NC: Duke University Press, 1–67.

Fitz-Gibbon, D. (2018). *Marketable Values: Inventing the Property Market in Modern Britain*, Chicago: University of Chicago Press.

Fligstein, N. and Goldstein, A. (2010). The Anatomy of the Mortgage Securitization Crisis. In M. Lounsbury and P. M. Hirsch, eds., *Markets on Trial: The Economic Sociology of the US Financial Crisis, Part A*, Bingley: Emerald, 29–70.

Fogelson, R. M. (2013). *The Great Rent Wars: New York, 1917–1929*, New Haven: Yale University Press.

Föllmer, M. and Smith, M. B. (2015). Urban Societies in Europe since 1945: Toward a Historical Interpretation. *Contemporary European History*, 24 (4), 475–491.

Forsell, H. (2006). *Property, Tenancy, and Urban Growth in Stockholm and Berlin, 1860–1920*, Aldershot, UK: Ashgate.

Fourcaut, A. (2000). *La Banlieue en morceaux. La crise des lotissements défectueux en France dans l'entre-deux-guerres*, Grâne: Créaphis.

Frank, Z. (2018). Urban Property in Nineteenth-Century Rio de Janeiro: Rent, Neighborhoods, and Networks. In I. Gregory, D. DeBats and D. Lafreniere, eds., *The Routledge Companion to Spatial History*, London: Routledge, 544–566.

French, R. A. and Hamilton, F. E. I., eds. (1979). *The Socialist City: Spatial Structure and Urban Policy*, Chichester: Wiley.

Freund, D. (2007). *Colored Property: State Policy and White Racial Politics in Suburban America*, Chicago: University of Chicago Press.

Friendly, M. (2008). The Golden Age of Statistical Graphics. *Statistical Science*, 23(4), 502–535.

Gandy, M. (2004). Rethinking Urban Metabolism: Water, Space and the Modern City. *City*, 8(3), 363–379.

Gaudin, J-P. (1985). *L'avenir en plan. Technique et politique dans la prévision urbaine, 1900–1930*, Seyssel, France: Editions du Champ Vallon.

Geyer, M. and Bright, C. (1995). World History in a Global Age. *The American Historical Review*, 100(4), 1034–1060.

Gharney, I. (2012). The Real Estate Development Industry. In R. Crane and R. Weber, eds., *The Oxford Handbook of Urban Planning*, Oxford: Oxford University Press, 722–738.

Ghazaleh, P. (2017). Closed Markets? Creating Communities, Personalizing Property in Late Ottoman Egypt. *Quaderni Storici*, 52(1), 107–126.

Glaeser, E. (2013). A Nation of Gamblers: Real Estate Speculation and American History. NBER Working Paper 18825. Accessed 12 November 2019. https://www.nber.org/papers/w18825.pdf.

Glotzer, P. (2020). *How the Suburbs Were Segregated: Developers and the Business of Exclusionary Housing, 1890–1960*, New York: Columbia University Press.

Goldman, M. (2011). Speculative Urbanism and the Making of the Next World City. *International Journal of Urban and Regional Research*, 35(3), 555–581.

Goldstein, B. (2017). *The Roots of Urban Renaissance: Gentrification and the Struggle over Harlem*, Cambridge, MA: Harvard University Press.

Gotham, K. F. (2002). *Race, Real Estate, and Uneven Development: The Kansas City Experience, 1900–2000*, Albany: SUNY Press.

(2006). The Secondary Circuit of Capital Reconsidered: Globalization and the US Real Estate Sector. *American Journal of Sociology*, 112(1), 231–275.

Gray, N., ed. (2018). *Rent and its Discontents: A Century of Housing Struggle*, London: Rowan & Littlefield.

Green, D. R. and Owens, A. (2013). Geographies of Wealth: Real Estate and Personal Property Ownership in England and Wales, 1870 1902. *The Economic History Review*, 66(3), 848–872.

Greer, A. (2018). *Property and Dispossession: Natives, Empires and Land in Early Modern North America*, Cambridge: Cambridge University Press.

Grossi, P. (1981). *An Alternative to Private Property: Collective Property in the Juridical Consciousness of the Nineteenth Century*, translated by L. G. Cochrane, Chicago: University of Chicago Press.

Guha, R. (1963). *A Rule of Property for Bengal: An Essay on the Idea of Permanent Settlement*, Paris: Sorbonne.

Guldi, J. (2018). Global Questions about Rent and the Longue Durée of Urban Power, 1848 to the Present. *New Global Studies*, 12(1), 37–63.

Guyot, Y. (1885). *Lettres sur la politique coloniale*, Paris: C. Reinwald.

Haila, A. (1998). The Neglected Builder of Global Cities. In O. Källtorp, I. Elander, O. Ericsson and M. Franzen, eds., *Cities in Transformation, Transformation in Cities: Social and Symbolic Change of Urban Space*, Aldershot, UK: Ashgate, 51–64.

Halbwachs, M. (1909). *Les Expropriations et les prix des terrains à Paris (1860–1900)*, Paris: Publications de la Société Nouvelle de Librairie et d'Édition.

Hall, P. (2014). *Cities of Tomorrow: An Intellectual History of Urban Planning and Design since 1880*, 4th ed., Oxford: Wiley.

Harding, V. (2002). Space, Property, and Propriety in Urban England. *The Journal of Interdisciplinary History*, 32(4), 549–569.

Harris, R. (1996). *Unplanned Suburbs: Toronto's American Tragedy, 1900–1950*, Baltimore: Johns Hopkins University Press.

(2012). *Building a Market: The Rise of the Home Improvement Industry, 1914–1960*, Chicago: University of Chicago Press.

(2018). Modes of Informal Urban Development: A Global Phenomenon. *Journal of Planning Literature*, 33(3), 267–286.

Harris, R. and Lehrer, U., eds. (2018). *The Suburban Land Question: A Global Survey*, Toronto: University of Toronto Press.

Harris, R. and Vorms, C., eds. (2017). *What's in a Name?: Talking about Urban Peripheries*, Toronto: University of Toronto Press.

Harris, S. (2013). *Communism on Tomorrow Street: Mass Housing and Everyday Life after Stalin*, Baltimore, MD: Johns Hopkins University Press.

Hartog, H. (1983). *Public Property and Private Power: The Corporation of the City of New York in American Law, 1730–1870*, Chapel Hill, NC: University of North Carolina Press.

Harvey, D. (2008). The Right to the City. *New Left Review*, 53 (September-October). Accessed 19 February 2020. https://newleftreview.org/issues/II53/articles/david-harvey-the-right-to-the-city.

(2018). *The Limits to Capital*, rev. ed., London: Verso. First published 1982 by University of Chicago Press.

Haussmann, A. (1863). *Paris immobilier: Notions sur les placements en immeubles dans les zones parisiennes*, Paris: Amyot.

Hayden, D. (1981). *The Grand Domestic Revolution: A History of Feminist Designs for America's Homes, Neighborhoods, and Cities*, Cambridge, MA: MIT Press.

Hazareesingh, S. (2000). The Quest for Urban Citizenship: Civic Rights, Public Opinion, and Colonial Resistance in Early Twentieth-century Bombay. *Modern Asian Studies*, 34(4), 797–829.

(2001). Colonial Modernism and the Flawed Paradigms of Urban Renewal: Uneven Development in Bombay, 1900–25. *Urban History*, 28(2), 235–255.

Hein, C. (2010). Shaping Tokyo: Land Development and Planning Practice in the Early Modern Japanese Metropolis. *Journal of Urban History*, 36(4), 447–484.

Hentschel, C. (2015). Postcolonializing Berlin and the Fabrication of the Urban. *International Journal of Urban and Regional Research*, 39(1), 79–91.

Hernandez, K. (2010–2011). The Bungalow Boom: The Working-Class Housing Industry and the Development and Promotion of Early-Twentieth-Century Los Angeles. *South California Quarterly*, 92 (4), 351–392.

Hertweck, F. (2020). *Architecture on Common Ground: The Question of Land, Positions and Models*, Zurich: Lars Müller Publishers.

Herzog, T. (2015). *Frontiers of Possession: Spain and Portugal in Europe and the Americas*, Cambridge, MA: Harvard University Press.

Hirt, S. (2013). Whatever Happened to the (Post)Socialist City? *Cities*, 32(1), 29–38.

Home, R. (2013). *Of Planting and Planning: The Making of British Colonial Cities*, 2nd ed., London: Routledge.

Hopkins, A. G. (1980). Property Rights and Empire Building: Britain's Annexation of Lagos, 1861. *Journal of Economic History*, 40(4), 777–98.

Hoppit, J. (2011). Compulsion, Compensation, and Property Rights in Britain, 1688–1833. *Past and Present*, 210, 93–128.

Hornstein, J. M. (2005). *A Nation of Realtors: A Cultural History of the Twentieth-Century American Middle Class*, Durham, NC: Duke University Press.

Hosagrahar, J. (2005). *Indigenous Modernities: Negotiating Architecture and Urbanism*, London: Routledge.

Hoyt, H. (1933). *One Hundred Years of Land Values in Chicago: The Relationship of the Growth of Chicago to the Rise of Its Land Values, 1830–1933*, Chicago: University of Chicago Press.

Hugill, H. (2017). What Is a Settler-Colonial City? *Geography Compass*, 11(5), 1–11.

Isamoglu, H., ed. (2004). *Constituting Modernity: Private Property in the East and West*, London: I. B. Tauris.

(2004). Politics of Administering Property: Law and Statistics in the Nineteenth-Century Ottoman Empire. In H. Isamoglu, ed., *Constituting Modernity: Private Property in the East and West*, London: I. B. Tauris, 276–320.

Issar, S. (2017). Codes of Contention: Building Regulations in Colonial Bombay, 1870–1912. *Journal of Historical Sociology*, 30(2), 164–188.

Jackson, K. (1985). *Crabgrass Frontier: The Suburbanization of the United States*, Oxford: Oxford University Press.

Jacobs, J. (2015). *Detached America: Building Houses in Postwar Suburbia*, Charlottesville, VA: University of Virginia Press.

Jacquot, S. and Morelle, M. (2018). Comment penser l'informalité dans les villes « du Nord », à partir des théories urbaines « du Sud »? *Métropoles*, 22. Accessed 3 February 2020. https://doi.org/10.4000/metropoles.5601.

Jakes, A. (2020). *Egypt's Occupation: Colonial Economism and the Crises of Capitalism*, Stanford: Stanford University Press.

Jindrich, J. (2017). Squatting in the US: What Historians Can Learn from Developing Countries. In F. Anders and A. Sedlmaier, eds., *Public Goods versus Economic Interests: Global Perspectives on the History of Squatting*, London: Routledge, 56–77.

Kaika, M. and Ruggiero, L. (2013). Land Financialization as a Lived Process: The Transformation of Milan's Bicocca by Pirelli. *European Urban and Regional Studies*, 23(1), 3–22.

Kang, Z. (1993). L'immobilier au XIXe siècle en France: Entre statistique et fiscalité. *Revue d'économie financière*, numéro hors-série, 71–86.

Karr, R. D. (2015). Suburban Land Development in Antebellum Boston. *Journal of Urban History*, 41(5), 862–880.

Kefford, A. (2020). Actually Existing Managerialism: Planning, Politics, and Property Development in Post-1945 Britain. *Urban Studies* (September). https://doi.org/10.1177/0042098020949034.

Kidambi, P. (2007). *The Making of an Indian Metropolis: Colonial Governance and Public Culture in Bombay, 1890–1920*, London: Routledge.

King, A. (1976). *Colonial Urban Development: Culture, Social Power, and Environment*, New York: Routledge.

  (2005). *The Bungalow: The Production of a Global Culture*, 2nd ed., Oxford: Oxford University Press.

Kingston, R. (2012). Capitalism in the Streets: Paris Shopkeepers, Passages Couverts, and the Production of the Early-Nineteenth-Century City. *Radical History Review*, 114, 39–65.

Klemek, C. (2011). *The Transatlantic Collapse of Urban Renewal: Postwar Urbanism from New York to Berlin*, Chicago: University of Chicago Press.

Knoll, K., Schularick, M. and Steger, T. (2014). No Place Like Home: Global House Prices, 1870–2012. CESifo Working Paper, No. 5006. Accessed 29 January 2020. http://hdl.handle.net/10419/103123.

Knox, P. L. (1991). The Restless Urban Landscape: Economic and Sociocultural Change and the Transformation of Metropolitan Washington, DC. *Annals of the Association of American Geographers*, 81(2), 181–209.

Kuchta, T. (2010). *Semi-Detached Empire: Suburbia and the Colonization of Britain, 1880 to the Present*, Charlottesville, VA: University of Virginia Press.

Kusiak, J. (2019). Legal Technologies of Primitive Accumulation: Judicial Robbery and Dispossession-by-Restitution in Warsaw. *International Journal of Urban and Regional Research*, 43(4), 649–665.

Kwak, N. (2015). *A World of Homeowners: American Power and the Politics of Housing Aid*, Chicago: University of Chicago Press.

(2021). Urban Informality in the Global North: A View from Los Angeles. *Esboços*, 28 (47), 182-196.

Lands, L. (2002). Speculators Attention! Workers and Rental Housing Development in Atlanta, 1880 to 1910. *Journal of Urban History*, 28(5), 546–572.

(2009). *The Culture of Property: Race, Class, and Housing Landscapes in Atlanta, 1880–1950*, Athens: University of Georgia Press.

Lasner, M. (2012). *High Life: Condo Living in the Suburban Century*, New Haven, CT: Yale University Press.

Latham, M. (2017). A Fraud, a Drunkard, and a Worthless Scamp: Estate Agents, Regulation, and Realtors in the Interwar Period. *Business History*, 59(5), 690-709.

Lear, J. (1996). Mexico City: Space and Class in the Porfirian Capital, 1884–1910. *Journal of Urban History*, 22(4), 454–492.

Lee, M. and Weiss, S. (2020). Cities on Paper: On the Materiality of Paper in Urban Planning. *Journal of Urban History*, 46(2), 239–247.

Lee, Y.-H. (2014). Land Reform and Colonial Land Legislation in Korea, 1894–1910. *Korea Journal*, 54(3), 126–149.

Lees, A. (1985). *Cities Perceived: Urban Society in American and European Thought, 1820–1940*, Manchester: Manchester University Press.

Lees, L. H. (2015). Michael B. Katz's 'From Site to Place' and Urban History in Europe and Beyond. *Journal of Urban History*, 41(4), 592–595.

Lefebvre, H. (2003 [1973]). *The Urban Revolution*, Minneapolis: University of Minnesota Press.

Lescure, M. (1980). *Les sociétés immobilières en France au XIXe siècle – Contribution à l'histoire de la mise en valeur du sol urbain en économie capitaliste*, Paris: Publications de la Sorbonne.

Levy, J. (2013). The Mortgage Worked the Hardest: The Fate of Landed Independence in Nineteenth-Century America. In M. Zakim and G. J. Kornblith, eds., *Capitalism Takes Command: The Social Transformation of Nineteenth-Century America*, Chicago: University of Chicago Press, 39–67.

Lewinnek, E. (2010). Mapping Chicago, Imagining Metropolises: Reconsidering the Zonal Model of Urban Growth. *Journal of Urban History*, 36(2), 197–220.

(2014). *The Working Man's Reward: Chicago's Early Suburbs and the Roots of American Sprawl*, Oxford: Oxford University Press.

Loeb, C. (2001). *Entrepreneurial Vernacular: Developers' Subdivisions in the 1920s*, Baltimore: Johns Hopkins University Press.

Logan, J. and Molotch, H. (1987). *Urban Fortunes: The Political Economy of Place*, Berkeley: University of California Press.

Łozowksi, P. (2018). The Social Structure of the Real Estate Market in Old Warsaw in the Years 1427–1527. *Economic History of Developing Regions*, 33(2), 147–182.

Macauley, M. (2001). A World Made Simple: Law and Property in the Ottoman and Qing Empires. *Journal of Early Modern History*, 5(4), 331–352.

Maggor, N. (2017). *Brahmin Capitalism: Frontiers of Wealth and Populism in Americas First Gilded Age*, Cambridge, MA: Harvard University Press.

Magri, S. (1996). Les propriétaires, les locataires, la loi: Jalons pour une analyse sociologique des rapports de location, Paris 1850–1920. *Revue française de sociologie*, 37(3), 397–418.

Maier, C. S. (2016). *Once Within Borders: Territories of Power, Wealth, and Belonging since 1500*, Cambridge, MA: Harvard University Press.

Mann, K. (2007). *Slavery and the Birth of an African City: Lagos, 1760–1900*, Bloomington: Indiana University Press.

Marcinkoski, C. (2015). *The City that Never Was*, New York: Princeton Architectural Press.

Marcus, S. (1999). *Apartment Stories: City and Home in Nineteenth-Century Paris and London*, Berkeley: University of California Press.

Marcuse, P. (1996). Privatization and its Discontents: Property Rights in Land and Housing in the Transition in Eastern Europe. In G. Andrusz, M. Harloe and I. Szelenyi, eds., *Cities After Socialism: Urban and Regional Change and Conflict in Post-Socialist Societies*, Oxford: Blackwell, 119–191.

Massard-Guilbaud, G. and Thorsheim, P. (2007). Cities, Environments, and European History. *Journal of Urban History*, 33(5), 691–701.

Matthews, G. (2011). *Ghetto at the Center of the World: Chungking Mansions, Hong Kong*, Chicago: University of Chicago Press.

McDonald, D. (2019). The Origins of Informality in a Brazilian Planned City: Belo Horizonte, 1889–1900. *Journal of Urban History*, 47(1), 29–49.

McFarlane, L. (1987). Nativism or Not? Perceptions of British Investment in Kansas, 1882–1901. *Great Plains Quarterly*, 7(4), 232–243.

Michel, H. (2006). *La Cause des propriétaires. État et propriété en France, fin XIXe – XXe siècle*, Paris: Belin.

Middell, M. and Naumann, K. (2010). Global History and the Spatial Turn: From the Impact of Area Studies to the Study of Critical Junctures of Globalization. *Journal of Global History*, 5(1), 149–170.

Ministère du commerce, de l'industrie, et des colonies (1889). *Congrès international pour l'étude de la transmission de la propriété foncière*, Paris: Imprimerie Nationale.

Monchow, H. C. (1928). *The Use of Deed Restrictions in Subdivision Development*, Chicago: Institute for Research in Land Economics.

Moore, J. W. (2015). *Capitalism in the Web of Life: Ecology and the Accumulation of Capital*, London: Verso Books.

Morales, M. (1975). Concentration of Urban Property Ownership: Sources and Analytical Perspectives, 1813–1900. *Latin American Research Review*, 10 (2), 125–127.

Morgan, N. J. and Daunton, M. (1983). Landlords in Glasgow: A Study of 1900. *Business History*, 25(3), 264–286.

Muller, E. K. and Tarr, J. A. (2019). The Interaction of Natural and Built Environments in the Pittsburgh Landscape. In E. K. Muller and J. A. Tarr, eds., *Making Industrial Pittsburgh Modern: Environment, Landscape, Transportation, and Planning*, Pittsburgh: University of Pittsburgh Press, 11–48.

Mulvey, M. (2016). The Problem that had a Name: French High-Rise Developments and the Fantasy of a Suburban Homemaker Pathology, 1954–1973. *Gender and History*, 28, 177–198.

Mundy, M. (2004). The State of Property: Late Ottoman Southern Syria, the Kazâ of Ajlun (1875–1918). In H. Isamoglu, ed., *Constituting Modernity: Private Property in the East and West*, London: I. B. Tauris, 214–247.

Murphy, E. (2015). *For a Proper Home: Housing Rights in the Margins of Urban Chile, 1960–2010*, Pittsburgh: University of Pittsburgh Press.

Murphy, E. and Hourani, N. B. (2013). *The Housing Question: Tensions, Continuities, and Contingencies in the Modern City*, Burlington, VT: Ashgate.

Myers, G. A. (2003). *Verandahs of Power: Colonialism and Space in Urban Africa*, Syracuse: Syracuse University Press.

Nasiali, M. (2016). *Native to the Republic: Empire, Social Citizenship, and Everyday Life in Marseille since 1945*, Ithaca, NY: Cornell University Press.

Newman, K. (2009). Post-Industrial Widgets: Capital Flows and the Production of the Urban. *International Journal of Urban and Regional Research*, 33 (3), 314–331.

Nightingale, C. (2012). *Segregation: A Global History of Divided Cities*, Chicago: University of Chicago Press.

O'Donnell, A. (2014). A Noah's Ark: Material Life and the Foundations of Soviet Governance, 1916–1922, unpublished PhD dissertation, Princeton University.

Offer, A. (1981). *Property and Politics, 1870–1914: Landownership, Law, Ideology and Urban Development in England*, Cambridge: Cambridge University Press.

Peck, J., Theodore, N. and Brenner, N. (2009). Neoliberal Urbanism: Models, Moments, Mutations. *SAIS Review*, 29(1), 49–66.

Pellandini-Simányi, L., Hammer, F. and Vargha, Z. (2015). The Financialization of Everyday Life or the Domestication of Finance?: How Mortgages Engage with Borrowers' Temporal Horizons, Relationships, and Rationality in Hungary. *Cultural Studies*, 29(5–6), 733–759.

Peñalver, E. M. (2008–2009). Land Virtues. *Cornell Law Review*, 94, 821–888.

(2011). Property's Memories. *Fordham Law Review*, 80, 1071–1088.

Perlman, J. (1976). *The Myth of Marginality: Urban Poverty and Politics in Rio de Janeiro*, Berkeley: University of California Press.

(2004). Marginality: From Myth to Reality in the Favelas of Rio de Janeiro, 1969–2002. In A. Roy and N. AlSayyad, eds., *Urban Informality: Transnational Perspectives from the Middle East, Latin America, and South Asia*, Lanham, MD: Lexington Books, 105–146.

Phelps, N., ed. (2017). *Old Europe, New Suburbanization?: Governance, Land, and Infrastructure in European Suburbanization*, Toronto: University of Toronto Press.

Picon, A. (2003). Nineteenth-Century Urban Cartography and the Scientific Ideal: The Case of Paris. *Osiris*, 18, 135–149.

Piketty, T. (2014). *Capital in the Twenty-First Century*, Cambridge, MA: Harvard University Press.

Pinto, P. R. (2009). Housing and Citizenship: Building Social Rights in Twentieth-Century Portugal. *Contemporary European History*, 18(2), 199–215.

Pistor, K. (2019). *The Code of Capital: How the Law Creates Wealth and Inequality*, Princeton: Princeton University Press.

Porter, L. and Yiftachel, O. (2019). Urbanizing Settler-Colonial Studies: Introduction to the Special Issue. *Settler Colonial Studies*, 9(2), 177–186.

Priest, C. (2006). Creating an American Property Law: Alienability and Its Limits in American History. *Harvard Law Review*, 120(2), 385–459.

Procès-verbaux de la commission chargée de faire une enquête sur la situation des ouvriers de l'industrie et de l'agriculture en France et de présenter un premier rapport sur la crise industrielle à Paris (1884). *Annales de la Chambre des Députés, Documents Parlementaires*, 12, Paris, n.p.

Prochaska, D. (2004). *Making Algeria French: Colonialism in Bône, 1870–1920*, Cambridge: Cambridge University Press.

Raff, D., Wachter, S. and Yan, S. (2013). Real Estate Prices in Beijing, 1644–1840. *Explorations in Economic History*, 50(3), 368–386.

Rao, N. (2012). Uncertain Ground: The Ownership Flat and Urban Property in Twentieth-Century Bombay. *South Asian History and Culture*, 3(1), 1–25.

(2013). *House, but No Garden: Apartment Living in Bombay's Suburbs, 1898–1964*, Minneapolis: University of Minnesota Press.

Reese, C. M. (2002). The Urban Development of Mexico City, 1850–1930. In A. Almandoz, ed., *Planning Latin Americas Capital Cities, 1850–1950*, London: Routledge, 139–169.

Ribeiro, L. C. de Q. (1989). The Constitution of Real Estate Capital and Production of Built-Up Space in Rio de Janeiro, 1870–1930. *International Journal of Urban and Regional Research*, 13(1), 47–67.

Robinson, J. (2006). *Ordinary Cities: Between Modernity and Development*, Routledge: London.

Rodger, R. (2002). *The Transformation of Edinburgh: Land, Property, and Trust in the Nineteenth Century*, Cambridge: Cambridge University Press.

Rodgers, D. T. (1998). *Atlantic Crossings: Social Politics in a Progressive Age*, Cambridge, MA: Harvard University Press.

Rolnik, R. (2013). Late Neoliberalism: The Financialization of Homeownership and Housing Rights. *International Journal of Urban and Regional Research*, 37(3), 1058–1066.

Roncayolo, M. (2002). *Lectures de villes: Formes et Temps*, rev. ed., Marseille. Éditions Parenthèses.

Roy, A. (2005). Urban Informality: Toward an Epistemology of Planning. *Journal of the American Planning Association*, 71(2), 147–158.

(2011). Slumdog Cities: Rethinking Subaltern Urbanism. *International Journal of Urban and Regional Research*, 35(2), 223–238.

(2012). Urban Informality: The Production of Space and the Practice of Planning. In R. Crane and R. Weber, eds., *The Oxford Handbook of Urban Planning*, Oxford: Oxford University Press, 691–705.

(2016). What is Urban about Critical Urban Theory? *Urban Geography*, 37 (6), 819–823.

(2017). Dis/possessive collectivism: Property and Personhood at City's End. *Geoforum*, 80, A1–A11.

Roy, A. and AlSayyad, N., eds. (2004). *Urban Informality: Transnational Perspectives from the Middle East, Latin America, and South Asia*, Lanham, MD: Lexington Books.

Rubin, E. (2012). *Insuring the City: the Prudential Center and the Postwar Urban Landscape*, New Haven, CT: Yale University Press.

Rudolph, N. (2015). *At Home in Postwar France: Modern Mass Housing and the Right to Comfort*, New York: Berghahn.

Rutheiser, C. (2003). Capitalizing on Havana: The Return of the Repressed in a Late Socialist City. In G. Bridge and S. Watson, eds., *A Companion to the City*, Blackwell: Oxford, 224–236.

Sand, J. (2005). *House and Home in Modern Japan: Architecture, Domestic Space, and Bourgeois Culture*, Cambridge, MA: Harvard University Press.

Sandoval-Strausz, A. K. and Kwak, N. H., eds. (2017). *Making Cities Global: The Transnational Turn in Urban History*, Philadelphia: University of Pennsylvania Press.

Sassen, S. (1994). *Global City*, Princeton: Princeton University Press.

(2008). Mortgage Capital and Its Particularities: A New Frontier for Global Finance. *Journal of International Affairs*, 62(1), 187–212.

(2014). *Expulsions: Brutality and Complexity in the Global Economy*, Cambridge, MA: Harvard University Press.

Satter, B. (2009). *Family Properties: Race, Real Estate, and the Exploitation of Black Urban America*, New York: Metropolitan Books.

Schwartz, V. (2001). Walter Benjamin for Historians. *The American Historical Review*, 106(5), 1721–1743.

Searle, L. G. (2016). *Landscapes of Accumulation: Real Estate and the Neoliberal Imagination in Contemporary India*, Chicago: University of Chicago Press.

Serban, M. (2019). *Subverting Communism in Romania: Law and Private Property, 1945–1965*, Lanham, MD: Lexington Books.

Shapely, P. (2013). Governance in the Post-war City: Historical Reflections on Public-Private Partnerships in the UK. *International Journal of Urban and Regional Research*, 37(4), 1288–1304.

Shapiro, A. (1985). *Housing the Poor of Paris, 1850–1902*, Madison: University of Wisconsin Press.

Sheinbaum, D. (2010). Gated Communities in Mexico City: A Historical Perspective. In S. Bagaeen, O. Uduku, eds., *Gated Communities: Social Sustainability in Contemporary and Historical Gated Developments*, London: Routledge, 79–91.

Shawkat, Y. (2020). *Egypt's Housing Crisis: The Shaping of Urban Space*, New York: The American University in Cairo Press.

Sheppard, E., Gidwani, V., Goldman, M., Leitner, H., Roy, A. and Maringanti, A. (2015). Introduction: Urban Revolutions in the Age of Global Urbanism. *Urban Studies* 52(11), 1947–1961.

Shiller, R. (2005). *Irrational Exuberance*, 2nd ed., Princeton: Princeton University Press.

Sims, D. (2010). *Understanding Cairo: The Logic of a City Out of Control*, New York: The American University in Cairo Press.

Smith, M. B. (2010). *Property of Communists: The Urban Housing Program from Stalin to Khrushchev*, Dekalb, IL: Northern Illinois University Press.

Smith, N. (1996). *New Urban Frontier: Gentrification and the Revanchist City*, New York: Routledge.

(2002). New Globalism, New Urbanism: Gentrification as Global Urban Strategy. *Antipode*, 34(3), 427–450.

Stevens, S. (2016). *Developing Expertise: Architecture and Real Estate in Metropolitan America*, New Haven, CT: Yale University Press.

Stout, N. (2019). *Dispossessed: How Predatory Bureaucracy Foreclosed on the American Middle Class*, Oakland, CA: University of California Press.

Stovall, T. (2012). *Paris and the Spirit of 1919 : Consumer Struggles, Transnationalism, and Revolution*, Cambridge: Cambridge University Press.

Surkis, J. (2019). *Sex, Law, and Sovereignty in French Algeria, 1830–1930*, Ithaca, NY: Cornell University Press.

Taylor, K.-Y. (2019). *Race for Profit: Black Homeownership and the End of the Urban Crisis*, Chapel Hill, NC: University of North Carolina Press.

Taylor, V. and Trentmann, F. (2011). Liquid Politics: Water and the Politics of Everyday Life in the Modern City. *Past and Present*, 211, 199–241.

Tejani, S (2020). Disputing 'Market Value': The Bombay Improvement Trust and the Reshaping of a Speculative Land Market in Early Twentieth-Century Bombay. *Urban History*. Accessed 6 February 2021. Advance online publication. https://doi.org/10.1017/S0963926820000565.

Tomiak, J. (2017). Contesting the Settler City: Indigenous Self-Determination, New Urban Reserves, and the Neoliberalization of Colonialism. *Antipode*, 49(4), 928–945.

Tonkiss, F. (2005). *Space, the City, and Social Theory*, Oxford: Wiley.

Topalov, C., ed. (1999). *Laboratoires du Nouveau Siècle: La nebuleuse reformatrice et ses réseaux en France, 1880–1914*, Paris: Editions de l'Ecole des Hautes Etudes en Sciences Sociales.

(2006). Maurice Halbwachs et les sociologues de Chicago. *Revue française de sociologie*, 47(3), 561–590.

Topalov, C., Coudroy de Lille, L., Depaule, J.-C. and Marin, B., eds. (2010). *L'aventure des mots de la ville à travers le temps, les langues, les sociétés*, Paris: Robert Laffont.

Topik, S. C. and Wells, A. (2012). *Global Markets Transformed, 1870–1945*. Cambridge, MA: Harvard University Press.

Tzaninis, Y., Mandler, T., Kaika, M. and Keil, R. (2021). Moving Urban Political Ecology beyond the 'Urbanization of Nature'. *Progress in Human Geography*, 45(2), 229–252.

Vanaik, A. (2019). *Possessing the City: Property and Politics in Delhi, 1911–1947*. Oxford: Oxford University Press.

Vasudevan, A. (2017). *The Autonomous City: A History of Urban Squatting*, London: Verso.

Veracini, L. (2012). Suburbia, Settler Colonialism, and the World Turned Inside Out. *Housing, Theory, and Society*, 29(4), 339–357.

Verdery, K. (2003). *The Vanishing Hectare: Property and Value in Postsocialist Transylvania*, Ithaca, NY: Cornell University Press.

Verlaan, T. (2019). Producing Space: Post-war Redevelopment as Big Business: Utrecht and Hannover 1962–1975. *Planning Perspectives*, 34(3), 415–437.

(2020). The Neues Kreuzberger Zentrum: Urban Planners, Property Developers and Fractious Left Politics in West Berlin, 1963–1974. *German History*, 38(1), 113–132.

Wacquant, L. (2008). *Urban Outcasts: A Comparative Sociology of Advanced Marginality*, Cambridge: Polity Press.

Wakeman, R. (2016). *Practicing Utopia: An Intellectual History of the New Town Movement*, Chicago: University of Chicago Press.

Ward, C. (2002). *Cotters and Squatters: Housing's Hidden History*. Nottingham, UK: Five Leaves.

Warner Jr, S. B. (1968). *The Private City: Philadelphia in Three Periods of Its Growth*, Philadelphia: University of Pennsylvania Press.

(1978). *Streetcar Suburbs: The Process of Growth in Boston, 1870–1900*, Cambridge, MA: Harvard University Press.

Weaver, J. (2003). *The Great Land Rush and the Making of the Modern World, 1650–1900*, Kingston, ON: McGill-Queens University Press.

Weinstein, L. (2008). Mumbai's Development Mafias: Globalization, Organized Crime and Land Development. *International Journal of Urban and Regional Research*, 32(1), 22–39.

Weiss, M. (1987). *Rise of the Community Builders: The American Real Estate Industry and Urban Land Planning*, New York City: Columbia University Press.

(2000). James A. Graaskamp, Richard T. Ely, and the Tradition of Real Estate and Urban Land Economics at the University of Wisconsin. In J. R. DeLisle and E. M. Worzala, eds., *Essays in Honor of James A. Graaskamp: Ten Years After*, Boston, MA: Springer, 323–339.

White, E., Snowden, K. and Fishback, P. V. (2014). *Housing and Mortgage Markets in Historical Perspective*, Chicago: University of Chicago Press.

Wright, G. (1983). *Building the Dream: A Social History of Housing in America*, Cambridge, MA: MIT Press.

(1991). *The Politics of Design in French Colonial Urbanism*, Chicago: University of Chicago Press.

Wyly, E., Atia, M., Foxcroft, H., Hammel, D. J. and Phillips-Watts, K. (2006). American Home: Predatory Mortgage Capital and Neighbourhood Spaces of Race and Class Exploitation in the United States. *Geografiska Annaler: Series B*, 88(1), 105–132.

Yates, A. (2011). Selling *la petite propriété*: Marketing Home Ownership in Early-Twentieth-Century Paris. *Entreprises et Histoire*, 64(3), 11–40.

(2012). Making Metropolitan Markets: Information, Intermediaries, and Real Estate in Modern Paris. In H. Berghoff and U. Spiekermann, eds., *Marketing and Market Research*, New York: Palgrave, 95–125.

(2015). *Selling Paris: Property and Commercial Culture in the Fin-de-siècle Capital*, Cambridge: Harvard University Press.

(2019a). Home-Making: Returnees, Squatters, and Planners in Postwar France. *Journal of Urban History*, 45(5), 1084–1088.

(2019b). The Double Life of Property: Mobilizing Land and Making Capitalism in Modern France. *Critical Historical Studies*, 6(2), 247–278.

Yates, M. (2013). The Market in Freehold Land, 1300–1509: The Evidence of Feet of Fines. *Economic History Review*, 66(2), 579–600.

Yeh, A. G.-O. and Wu, F. (1996). The New Land Development Process and Urban Development in Chinese Cities. *International Journal of Urban and Regional Research*, 20(2), 330–353.

Zarecor, K. (2011). *Manufacturing a Socialist Modernity: Housing in Czechoslovakia, 1945–1960*, Pittsburgh: University of Pittsburgh Press.

(2018). What Was So Socialist about the Socialist City? Second World Urbanity in Europe. *Journal of Urban History*, 44(1), 95–117.

Zukin, S. (1982). *Loft Living: Culture and Capital in Urban Change*, Baltimore: Johns Hopkins University Press.

Cambridge Elements ≡

Global Urban History

Printed in the United States
by Baker & Taylor Publisher Services